OUTDOOR FIX-IT 101

Projects You Really *Can* Do Yourself

STEVE WILLSON

**Creative Publishing
international**

CHANHASSEN, MINNESOTA
www.creativepub.com

Creative Publishing
international

Copyright © 2007
Creative Publishing international, Inc.
18705 Lake Drive East
Chanhassen, Minnesota 55317
1-800-328-3895
www.creativepub.com
All rights reserved

Printed in China
10 9 8 7 6 5 4 3 2 1

President/CEO: Ken Fund

Home Improvement Group

Publisher: Bryan Trandem
Senior Editor: Mark Johanson
Editor: Jennifer Gehlhar
Managing Editor: Tracy Stanley
Senior Design Manager: Brad Springer
Design Managers: Jon Simpson, Mary Rohl
Production Artist: Dave Schelitzche
Director of Photography: Tim Himsel
Lead Photographer: Steve Galvin
Photo Coordinators: Julie Caruso, Joanne Wawra
Shop Manager: Randy Austin
Production Assistants: Glenn Austin, John Webb
Production Managers: Laura Hokkanen,
   Linda Halls
Author: Steve Willson
Photography: Joel Schnell
Page Layout: Kari Johnston

Library of Congress
Cataloging-in-Publication Data

Willson, Steve,
  Outdoor fix-it 101 : projects you really can do
yourself / by Steve Willson.
     p. cm.
Black & Decker
  Summary: "Covers basic maintenance of the
home's exterior shell--its siding, foundation and
roof--as well as maintenance and repair of
driveways, walkways, fences, and other essen-
tial outdoor structures"--Provided by publisher.
  Includes index.
  ISBN-13: 978-1-58923-300-3 (soft cover)
  ISBN-10: 1-58923-300-X (soft cover)
  1. Dwellings--Maintenance and repair--
Amateurs' manuals. 2. Exterior walls--
Maintenance and repair--Amateurs' manuals. 3.
Sealing (Technology)--Amateurs' manuals. 4.
Garden structures--Maintenance and repair--
Amateurs' manuals. 5. Do-it-yourself work. I.
Title.

  TH4817.3.W555 2007
  643'.7--dc22

  2006034652

NOTICE TO READERS

For safety, use caution, care and good judgment when following the procedures described in this book. The Publisher and
Black & Decker cannot assume responsibility for any damage
to property or injury to persons as a result of misuse of the
information provided.

The techniques shown in this book are general techniques for
various applications. In some instances, additional techniques
not shown in this book may be required. Always follow manufacturers' instructions included with products, since deviating
from the directions may void warranties. The projects in this
book vary widely as to skill levels required: some may not be
appropriate for all do-it-yourselfers, and some may require professional help.

Consult your local Building Department for information on
building permits, codes and other laws as they apply to your
project.

CONTENTS

Welcome to Outdoor Fix-it 101

THOUGH THEY'RE NOT ALWAYS THE FLASHIEST PROJECTS, REPAIRS TO THE EXTERIOR WALLS, THE ROOF, THE FOUNDATION, THE WINDOWS, SIDING AND DOORS ARE AMONG THE MOST IMPORTANT YOU CAN DO. NEGLECT THEM, AND YOUR HOUSE BECOMES AN EYE SORE TO THE NEIGHBORHOOD WAITING TO FALL APART; DO THEM DILIGENTLY AND YOUR HOME WILL BE A LIFETIME PARADISE FOR YOU AND YOUR FAMILY.

Well, that's probably exaggerating just a bit. But the reality is that keeping your home secure against wind and rain is what makes a comfortable life indoors possible. The siding, roof and walls that make up the thing we call "home" is what protects us and our families. It is our primary shelter that keeps us healthy and safe, the place that makes it possible to pursue that mysterious thing called happiness.

That's why so many of the projects in this book are aimed at sealing out the elements, or repairing damage caused by the wind, rain and sun. That's at the heart of almost every outdoor repair and maintenance project—preventing of fixing damage caused by the elements.

Like all books in the Black & Decker *101* series, this is a book that can help you even if you know nothing at all about home repairs or improvements. None of the projects is very complicated, and all the information you'll need to get each project done is found right here. You'll see all the tools and materials you'll need, and each step of the process is photographed so you'll know exactly what to do.

HERE'S HOW TO USE THIS BOOK:

The first two pages of each project give you the background information that will help you understand everything important about the project. Terms you need to know, tools and materials required, structural information about the project—it's all right here.

Then, turn the page to find detailed step-by-step instructions to accomplish the task at hand. Every step is photographed so there'll be no unanswered questions. And you'll also find helpful sidebars that anticipate unexpected problems, show how to use tools correctly, and give important safety tips.

We would like you to read the Orientation pages to learn just a little about some special safety practices that are important when working outdoors. But after studying these eight pages, you'll be prepared to take on any of the projects in this book.

It's that easy. Really.

Orientation:
The Great, Safe Outdoors

A LOT OF THE REPAIRS TO THE OUTSIDE OF YOUR HOME come with some inherent dangers, so it is very important that you read this section carefully before you start any project. Repairing roofing, siding, or gutters may mean that you have to climb ladders, for example. And some of the projects call for big powerful tools that you may not have experience with. And you may be working with glass and metal, which can be sharp enough to cut you....

Do we have your attention now? It's okay; relax. None of the projects in this book is really very dangerous, if you take your time, read up on the project carefully first, and use common sense as you go. If you follow the simple tips on these pages, you're virtually assured that your outdoor repairs will go like a charm.

The hazards in outdoor repairs can come from three sources. First, electricity can be just a little more hazardous in outdoor environments than indoors. That's because you're in close contact with the earth, which makes short circuits more likely. Fortunately, it's really pretty easy to avoid these hazards, by using a special safety device called a GFCI extension cord or outlet, or by using one of the many types of battery-powered tools now available.

The second hazard comes from using tools. Outdoor repairs may call for power tools, as well as some larger hand tools, and because outdoor projects sometimes offer more distractions, in the form of noise and weather, it's important to work carefully. Here are some things to keep in mind:

- Never work when you're tired. Working when well rested and alert will prevent most common accidents.

- Don't work alone if you can help it. Not only will many projects go easier with a helper, it will help to have someone there should an accident occur.

- Keep a phone handy, in case of emergencies.

- Work with good tools. Dull, worn-out tools invite accidents.

The third hazard is falling from ladders. This book includes some simple roofing and siding repairs that may require you to work on ladders. Here it's especially necessary to follow all the tips listed above. And make sure you pay attention to the ladder safety tips on the following pages.

Use cordless tools whenever possible, to free yourself from the hazards of working around corded power tools, which can get tangled, and are prone to be shock hazards.

Make yourself a tool platform by laying a piece of plywood on saw-horses. It's easy to lose tools in the grass, and keeping them elevated like this makes them easy to find and protects them from moisture.

Orientation:
Ladder Safety

Be very careful when working around power lines. Better yet, don't do it at all. If it's unavoidable, use only a wood or fiberglass ladder—never an aluminum ladder.

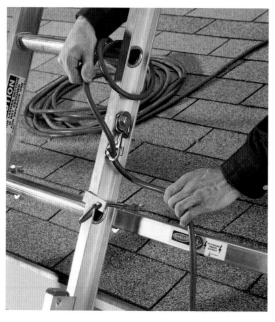

If you must work with power cords, attach a metal clip to the top of your ladder to tie off cords and keep them from entangling you on the ladder.

Wear sturdy boots, gloves, pants and shirts when working outdoors. A five gallon bucket equipped with a nylon organizing sleeve makes a lightweight carrier for toting tools up and down ladders.

A simple bracket called a ladder stabilizer gives broader support to a ladder leaning against a house, and makes it less likely to slip. The feet of the stabilizer should rest against a vertical surface, not on the roof.

Anchor the bottom of your ladder with stakes driven into the ground behind each foot of the ladder. If the ground is uneven, you can lay firm blocking under the legs to level the ladder.

HERE'S HOW

If your job requires a long time on a ladder, you'll find it easier if you rent or buy a pair of ladder jacks and a ladder plank to rest on a pair of extension ladders. Attach the jacks by slipping the rung mounts over the ladder rungs. Level the arms and lock them in place. Then set the plank in place on the platform arms, and adjust the ends of the jacks to hold the plank in place.

Orientation:
Your Outdoor Tool Kit

The outdoor fix-it projects in this book really don't require much in the way of special tools and materials. Although a few of the projects may call for a specialty tool or two, most of them can be completed with a basic set of hand and power tools.

The group of tools shown here is a collection that will put you well on your way to doing the projects in this book, as well as most general carpentry repair projects around the house. But don't worrry if you don't yet own them. You can gradually assemble your tool kit as you take on project after project. Or, you can borrow them from a neighbor or friend as you need them.

1 Fixing Clogged Gutters

Gutter systems play a critical role in protecting both the exterior and interior
of your house. By catching runoff water from the roof, gutters keep the
siding dry. They also prevent water from pooling around the foundation—
the most common cause of wet basements.

THE IDEA BEHIND GUTTERS IS SIMPLE: JUST COLLECT THE RAINWATER THAT FALLS ON A ROOF AND
DIVERT IT FROM THE FOUNDATION OF THE HOUSE. Ironically the root cause of gutter dys-
function is rarely the water itself. Instead it's the leaves and twigs that get trapped in the
gutters and clog the downspouts. When these exits are blocked, the water runs over the
lip of the gutter and falls exactly where you don't want it to fall: next to the foundation.
Clogged gutters lead to stained siding in the summer and ice dams in the winter. The
solution is obvious: clean the gutters a couple of times a year.

Cleaning gutters means working from ladders. To do the job right, lean an extension ladder against the house (with rubber ladder end guards to protect the siding) or against the
roof (using a ladder stabilizer). Climb up with a garden hose and bucket in hand. If
there's just a little bit of debris, try washing it out with the garden hose. But heavy con-
gestion has to be removed by hand. A putty knife is a good tool for this job. Just lift out
the mess and put it in the bucket. To free clogged downspouts, push a garden hose down
the pipe and run the water at full force until the clog breaks loose and the pipe is clear.

GUTTERS 101

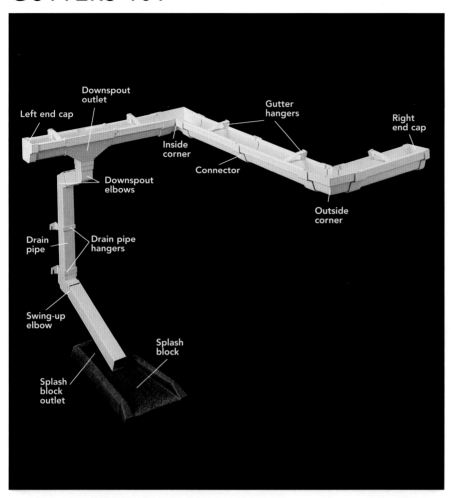

Clogs can occur anywhere in a gutter system, but the most likely trouble spots are at the downspout outlets and in the drain pipe.

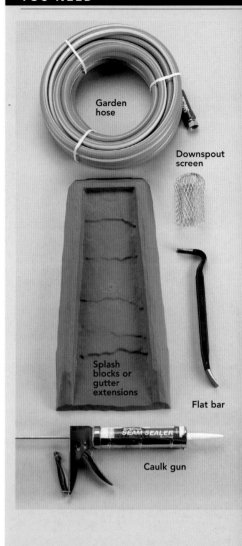

END CAPS—Placed at the end of gutter runs.

INSIDE/OUTSIDE CORNERS—Used on corners with no water outlet to carry water around a corner.

DOWNSPOUT OUTLETS—Should be placed at least every 35 feet.

DRAIN PIPE HANGERS—Should use at least two per drain pipe.

DOWNSPOUT ELBOWS—Recommended three per downspout.

This project can be completed in 4 to 6 hours.

HOW TO CLEAN & REPAIR CLOGGED GUTTERS

1 Clean dense debris from gutters using a putty knife or a narrow drywall knife. Put the debris in a bucket instead of dropping it on the ground.

2 Stubborn clogs in downspouts can be loosened and flushed away with a garden hose. Just push the end of the hose down the pipe and turn on the water full blast.

3 If your gutter collects a lot of leaves and frequently clogs the downspouts, slide a ball-shaped screen into the top of each pipe or cover the entire gutter with a protective screen.

4 Leaky joints between sections of gutter or at downspout connections can be patched with gutter seal. Just clean out any debris, dry the seam, and fill it well with sealer. Smooth the bead with your fingertip or a putty knife.

5 To straighten a sagging gutter, remove hangers or spikes in the sagging area. Snap a chalkline at the correct height, raise the gutter to the line, and then reinstall the hangers.

7 Splash blocks are designed to direct water from the downspouts away from the house foundation. If you have these blocks, make sure they're positioned directly under the downspouts. If you don't have the blocks, buy and install them.

6 To straighten gutters that are supported with hanging brackets, loosen the brackets, lift the gutter and reinstall the brackets.

FYI

A folding extension is a gutter accessory that mounts on the bottom on a downspout and works like a splash block to send the water away from the house. Because it's hinged, the pipe can be folded up out of the way when mowing or working in planting beds next to the house.

Touching Up
Exterior Paint

Few projects will go further than touching up painted siding when it comes to freshening up the appearance of your house.

IF YOU OWN A HOUSE WITH A PAINTED EXTERIOR, YOU ALREADY KNOW ABOUT PERPETUAL MAINTENANCE. It goes something like this. You painted your house the year your daughter graduated from eighth grade. It was a big deal because you had to get it done between her end-of-school party (in your backyard) and the family reunion in August (also in your backyard). Of course you spent your whole vacation doing it, except for the two days when nearly every in-law asked why you didn't hire a professional to do the job. Sometimes doing the right thing doesn't seem like the right thing to do.

But once the job was done, you enjoyed (for about three years) not thinking about paint. Then it started. At first it was just a little flaking along the bottom edge of the fascia. Then it spread to the window casing boards and the top edge of the water table, behind the bushes. Suddenly, it became clear that the whole house would need repainting just when your daughter would be graduating from high school. Talk about perpetual maintenance.

Unfortunately, there's no happy ending to this dark story. But there is a way to protect your flank while retreating: routine paint touch-ups. If you fix the little things when they go bad, you can easily postpone a major repainting for several years. And every summer without drop cloths and extension ladders is a blessing to be counted by all.

SANDING SIDING 101

Sanded to bare wood

Scraped and spot-sanded

Pressure-washed only

The amount of surface preparation you do will largely determine the final appearance of your paint job. Decide how much sanding and scraping you're willing to do to obtain a finish you'll be happy with.

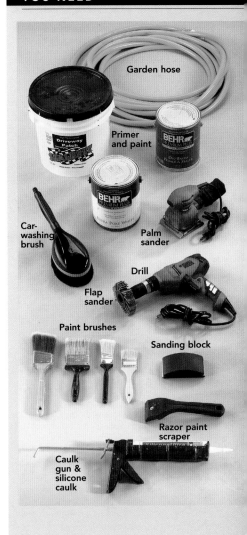

TERMS YOU NEED TO KNOW

CAR-WASHING BRUSH—A common automotive maintenance tool that consists of a soft-bristle brush mounted on the end of a wand made of aluminum tubing. The wand attaches to a garden hose.

FLAP SANDER—An accessory designed for electric drills made of narrow pieces of abrasive paper attached to a steel arbor. The drill turns the arbor and paper in a rotary motion.

1 Wash your siding with an inexpensive hose-mounted brush, such as a car-washing brush. Work from the top of the wall to the bottom. Use household detergent on tough spots and rinse all soapy areas thoroughly.

2 Scrape away peeling paint with a paint scraper. Don't gouge the wood, and be sure to change (or sharpen) the scraper blade frequently to make the work go faster.

3 Use 100-grit sandpaper over a sanding block to smooth the scraped areas. Feather the edges so they match the surrounding surface.

4 Use a flap sander mounted in an electric drill (or a cordless drill for very quick jobs) to remove peeling paint from curved surfaces. This tool works on both concave and convex boards.

5 On larger scraped areas, use an electric sander to smooth the surface. Use 100-grit sandpaper and be sure to brush the sanding dust off the siding or trim when you're done.

6 Fill any cracks between the siding and the door and window trim using a caulk gun and paintable, exterior caulk. Fill deep cracks in a couple of passes to keep the caulk from smearing on the siding.

7 Prime and then paint all sanded areas. And, try not to over-brush. Because paint tends to fade over time, your touch-ups will look brighter than the original paint covering. Keeping their size as small as possible will make them less noticeable.

8 Try to remove any paint splatters from window glass before they dry. Once the paint hardens it's much harder to remove.

Pestproofing Your House

They might be cute as a button or perfectly gruesome, but uninvited pests can do enormous damage to your home and need to be kept out.

IN THE END, IT MAY BE A SIMPLE QUESTION OF ETIQUETTE. If you invite pests into your house, you can't feel put out when they decide to accept. And, what constitutes an invitation? Well, lots of things, like holes that aren't caulked, chimneys without protective flue covers, damaged vent screening and so on. Of course, taking such a hard line is a little bit like blaming the victim. Is everybody really supposed to know where all the holes in the house are and be familiar with the travel patterns of all the local squirrels? Probably not, at least when it comes to the squirrels.

The most common entry points are small holes along the foundation and soffits, and sometimes next to windows and doors. These should all be filled with silicone acrylic caulk. Holes much wider than ¼ in. should be stuffed with caulk backer before caulking. Also fill any gaps around where phone, gas, cable, electric, water and other services enter the house. Once you are done filling the obvious gaps, look for evidence of infestation like animal droppings or nesting materials. Remove these and check the area for any entry points that you might have missed. If the rodents persist, you can fight back with spring-loaded death traps or Havahart-type traps that capture the animal so it can be released outside.

PESTPROOFING 101

The mudsill is the area formed by the foundation wall and the sill plates of your exterior walls. It is the most likely point of pest invasions and should be inspected (look for light coming in from outdoors) and caulked regularly.

GETTING THEM OUT WHEN THEY'RE IN

There are many hardware-store products designed to help you get rid of pests inside your house. For insects in the attic and basement, pesticide foggers are one option. These shouldn't be used around food prep areas or when anyone is in the house. The usual approach is to activate the fogger and then leave for a few hours. No matter which product you buy, follow the use instructions carefully.

Common roach and ant traps do capture a lot of pests, but will not solve the problem unless the source from outside is eliminated. The same is true of all sorts of mousetraps. If you've closed all the entry points that you can find, and you've trapped all the pests that should have been inside when you plugged the holes, then you need help. Call a reputable exterminator and let them handle the job.

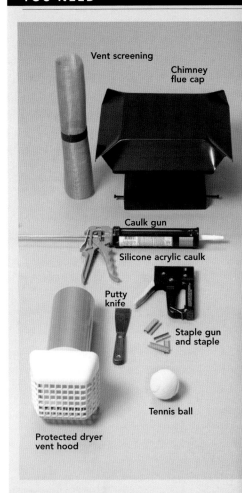

Vent screening

Chimney flue cap

Caulk gun

Silicone acrylic caulk

Putty knife

Staple gun and staple

Tennis ball

Protected dryer vent hood

DIFFICULTY LEVEL

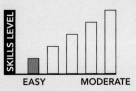

SKILLS LEVEL

EASY   MODERATE

This project can be completed in one to four hours.

HOW TO PESTPROOF YOUR HOUSE

1 If your chimney flue doesn't have a cap, you are inviting birds, bats, and squirrels into the flue, especially if you never use the fireplace. A chimney cap with screening or mesh on the sides will keep all these pests out.

2 Most roof vents come with screens installed to keep insects out of the house. If this screen is torn or missing, staple new screening (it's actually called insect mesh at the store) to the backside of the vent with ¼"-long staples.

3 Replace typical flap-type dryer vents (inset) with protected vent hoods. These keep out insects and small rodents, and are designed to be a universal replacement for standard vent hoods.

4 Sill plates are supposed to be installed over a sealer material that keeps out insects. But sometimes the sealer is left off. If you see evidence that insects are coming through the joint, fill it with caulk outside and inside (see page 21).

5 Insects can easily enter your house through a basement floor drain. The drain hole can be filled with a tennis ball that will float out of the way to allow water into the drain if the floor is flooded.

6 Check the foundation of your house for anthills, wasp's nests and termite tunnels. If you find any of these nests, remove them and close off the points of entry.

7 Be especially watchful in moist areas of the house where many insects prefer to be. Eliminate the access points and install a dehumidifier to make the area less attractive to pests.

8 If you ever find evidence of termite-eaten wood, call an exterminator immediately. These technicians can kill all the termites and check for other harmful species, like carpenter ants.

4

Repairing Stonework

Stones in a wall can become dislodged due to soil settling, erosion, or seasonal freeze-thaw cycles. Make the necessary repairs before the problem gets worse.

DAMAGE TO STONEWORK IS TYPICALLY CAUSED BY FROST HEAVE, EROSION OR DETERIORATION OF MORTAR, OR BY STONES THAT HAVE WORKED OUT OF PLACE. Dry-laid stone walls are more susceptible to erosion and popping, while mortared walls develop cracks that admit water, which can freeze and cause further damage.

Inspect stone structures once a year for signs of damage and deterioration. Replacing a stone or repointing crumbling mortar now will save you a lot of work in the long run.

A leaning stone column or wall probably suffers from erosion or foundation problems, and can be dangerous if neglected. If you have the time, you can tear down and rebuild dry-laid structures, but mortared structures with excessive lean need professional help.

STONE WALLS 101

A typical stone garden wall has at least one course below grade, often set on a base of gravel or crushed rock for drainage. The stones can be set in many patterns, but you'll usually find tie stones that are oriented perpendicular to the other stones, which strengthens the structure. A layer of flat rocks called cap stones is normal, especially on mortared walls.

TERMS YOU NEED TO KNOW

CAP STONE—The flat rocks laid as the top course of a stone wall.

TIE STONE—Stones that run the full width of a stone wall to help hold the wall together.

POINTING TROWEL—A small steel trowel with a pointed end that is used to place mortar into hard-to-reach areas.

TUCKPOINTING—The process of removing old, crumbling mortar and replacing it with fresh mortar.

TOOLS & SUPPLIES YOU NEED

DIFFICULTY LEVEL

This project can be completed in four to eight hours depending on the size of the wall.

HOW TO REPAIR A STONE WALL

1 Before you start, study the wall and determine how much of it needs to be rebuilt. Plan to dismantle the wall in a "V" shape, centered on the damaged section. Number each stone and mark its orientation with chalk so you can rebuild it following the original design. Tip: Photograph the wall, making sure the markings are visible.

2 Capstones are often set in a mortar bed atop the last course of stone. You may need to chip out the mortar with a maul and chisel to remove the capstones. Remove the marked stones, taking care to check the overall stability of the wall as you work.

3 Rebuild the wall, one course at a time, using replacement stones only when necessary. Start each course at the ends and work toward the center. On thick walls, set the face stones first, then fill in the center with smaller stones. Frequently check your work with a level as you progress. If your capstones were mortared, re-lay them in fresh mortar. Wash off the chalk with water and a stiff-bristle brush.

TIPS FOR REPLACING POPPED STONES

Return a popped stone to its original position. If other stones have settled in its place, drive shims between neighboring stones to make room for the popped stone. Be careful not to wedge too far.

Use a 2 × 4 covered with carpet to avoid damaging the stone when hammering it into place. After hammering, make sure a replacement stone hasn't damaged or dislodged the adjoining stones.

TIP FOR REPLACING A WALL SECTION

If you're rebuilding because of erosion, dig a trench at least 6" deep under the damaged area, and fill it with compactible gravel. Tamp the gravel with a hand tamper. This will improve drainage and prevent water from washing soil out from beneath the wall.

HOW TO REPAIR MORTARED JOINTS

1 Carefully rake out cracked and crumbling mortar, stopping when you reach solid mortar. Remove loose mortar and debris with a stiff-bristle brush. Tip: Rake the joints with a chisel and maul, or make your own raking tool by placing an old screwdriver in a vice and bending the shaft about 45°.

2 Mix dry mortar mix with water and bonding agent or acrylic fortifier, then dampen the repair surfaces with clean water. Working from the top down, pack mortar into the crevices, using a pointing trowel. Smooth the mortar when it has set up enough to resist light finger pressure. Remove excess mortar with a stiff-bristle brush.

TIPS FOR REPAIRING MORTARED STONE WALLS

Tint mortar for repair work so it blends with the existing mortar. Mix several samples of mortar, adding a different amount of tint to each, and allow them to dry. Compare each sample to the old mortar, and choose the closest match.

Use a mortar bag filled with fresh mortar to restore weathered and damaged mortar joints over an entire structure. Remove loose mortar and clean all surfaces with a stiff-bristle brush and water. Dampen the joints before tuckpointing, and cover all of the joints, smoothing and brushing as necessary.

1 Remove the damaged stone by chiseling out the surrounding mortar, using a masonry chisel or a modified screwdriver (previous page). Drive the chisel toward the damaged stone to avoid harming neighboring stones. Once the stone is out, chisel the surfaces inside the cavity as smooth as possible.

2 Brush out the cavity to remove loose mortar and debris. Test the surrounding mortar, and chisel or scrape or vacuum out any mortar that isn't firmly bonded.

3 Dry-fit the replacement stone. The stone should be stable in the cavity and blend with the rest of the wall. You can mark the stone with chalk and cut it to fit with a circular saw and masonry blade, but excessive cutting will result in a conspicuous repair.

4 Mist the stone and cavity lightly, then mix and apply fortified mortar around the inside of the cavity, using a pointing trowel. Also apply mortar to the replacement stone. Insert the stone and wiggle it forcefully to remove air pockets. Use the pointing trowel to pack additional mortar around the stone. Smooth the mortar once it has set up.

Fixing A Sliding Screen Door

5

Screen doors are extremely vulnerable to damage from feet, pets and a host of other hazards. But fixing them is a breeze.

SLIDING GLASS DOORS ARE MOSTLY GOOD THINGS. They let in a lot of light and when the sliding panel is open, they let in a lot of air. And, because all these doors have sliding screens, the air they let in is reasonably bug free. The problem is, the large screen easily falls victim to pets and children and often needs repair.

To replace the screen, you need to remove the screen door panel. It is held in grooves by four spring-loaded wheels, one at each corner of the door. It is nearly impossible, and very frustrating, to try to replace a screen with the panel in place. The screen is held in place with a flexible plastic spline cord which you can easily pull out.

Take a short section of the old spline to a hardware store or home center and buy new spline material that matches the diameter of the old one. Also buy replacement screening and an installation tool that is designed for the size of spline you are installing. These tools come with a roller on both ends. One is convex shaped and is used to forced the screen into the door groove. The other roller has a concave edge to force the spline over the screen.

WINDOW SCREENING 101

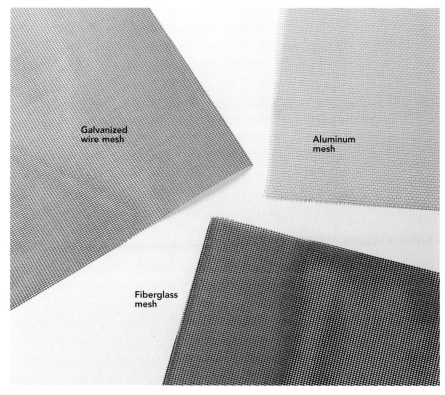

Galvanized wire mesh

Aluminum mesh

Fiberglass mesh

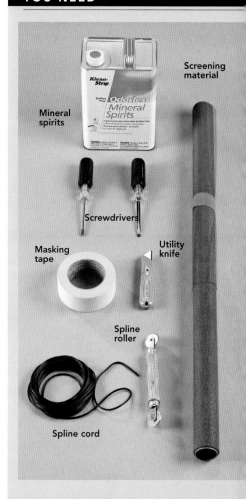

Mineral spirits

Screening material

Screwdrivers

Masking tape

Utility knife

Spline roller

Spline cord

Window screening (technically, it's called insect mesh) is woven from three different materials: galvanized wire, aluminum wire and black fiberglass strands. Each has its advantages and drawbacks: galvanized wire is inexpensive and easy to find, but can become misshapen or rusty; aluminum is less common, but it is strong and won't discolor as easily; fiberglass is easy to work with and won't rust or corrode, but it is prone to tearing. The best advice is simply to buy screening that matches the windows on the rest of your house.

TERMS YOU NEED TO KNOW

SPLINE—For sliding screen doors, a flexible plastic material (round in cross section) that holds screening tight in door grooves. Sold in long strings and sized to fit different width grooves.

SPLINE ROLLER—A specialty tool designed to force spline cords into the spline channel of the screen frame.

DIFFICULTY LEVEL

SKILLS LEVEL

EASY   MODERATE

This project can be completed in two to three hours.

HOW TO FIX A SLIDING SCREEN DOOR

1 You can't remove the screen door until you release the tension on the roller wheels. Back off the adjustment screws, then lift the door out of the channel that holds it captive.

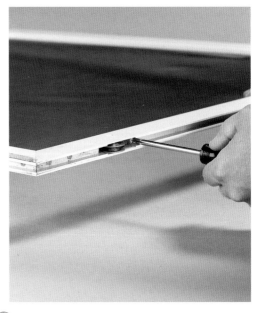

2 Remove the door rollers using a screwdriver. Sometimes these rollers can just be pried out. Other times you'll have to remove a small screw.

3 Clean the rollers with mineral spirits and an old paint brush. Once all the dirt and grime is removed, dry the rollers and lubricate them with light oil.

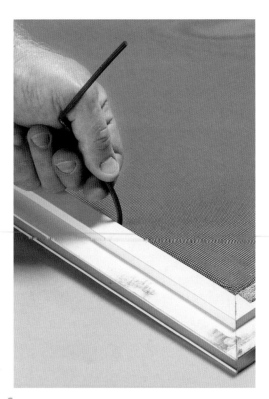

4 Pry up one corner of the old spline and then gently pull it out of the screen channel. If this plastic spline is still soft and flexible, it can be reused for the new screen.

5 Tape the new screen onto the door frame with masking tape. Then make a diagonal cut at each corner to remove the excess screen. This will keep the screen from bulging at the corner when it is pressed into its channel.

6 Force the screen into the door groove using the convex wheel on the spline roller installation tool. Don't force the screen in with a single pass. Rather, make several lighter passes until the screen reaches the bottom of the channel.

7 Once the screen is in the channel, install the spline material. Use the concave wheel and work slowly to make sure the spline is forced all the way into the channel. Several passes may be required.

8 Trim off any excess screening with a sharp utility knife. Do not cut the spline. Reinstall the wheels and replace the panel in the door.

Tuning Up
Double-Hung Windows

6

Double-hung windows stick from time to time and often are painted shut.
A special serrated paint tool is made for breaking the paint lines, but a
plain putty knife can also do the job.

DOUBLE-HUNG WINDOWS ARE THE MOST COMMON WINDOW TYPES. It's not hard to understand why. They don't open outward, which would expose them to more potential weather damage than they already confront. And, they don't open inward, which would tangle curtains and drapes every time you wanted some air. They don't have elaborate hinge mechanisms that wear over time and need service or replacement.

Newer models are much more energy efficient than older ones, and almost never need any maintenance beyond cleaning. Unfortunately, they don't look as good as older versions, unless you buy the top-drawer models. Many well-built windows still come with snap-in grills to simulate the muntins found on old sashes.

If you are have old windows and you want to keep them, know this: there will be some window maintenance in your future to keep things running smoothly.

DOUBLE-HUNG WINDOWS 101

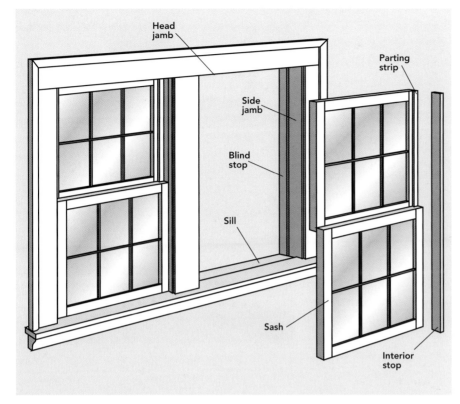

Head jamb

Parting strip

Side jamb

Blind stop

Sill

Sash

Interior stop

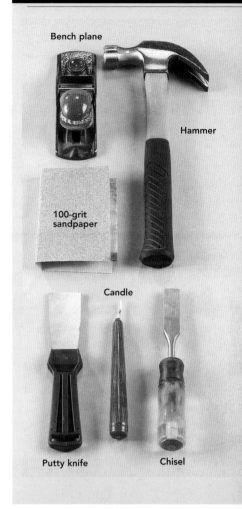

Bench plane

Hammer

100-grit sandpaper

Candle

Putty knife

Chisel

When they are working well, there's nothing like an old double-hung window. You can open and close a heavy sash with just one finger because the sashes are tied to counter weights that slide up and down in channels behind the side jambs. The balance between the weights and sash is so delicate that gentle finger pressure will start the weights moving down which will carry the sash up. Though the sash cords do break eventually, most poor performance is caused by binding sashes.

DIFFICULTY LEVEL

SKILLS LEVEL

EASY   MODERATE

This project can be completed in one to two hours per window.

TERMS YOU NEED TO KNOW

MUNTINS—Secondary framing members that hold multiple glass panes within a single window sash.

SASH STOP—A small trim board that is nailed to both window jambs to hold the sash in place. Also called a window stop.

PARTING STRIP—A narrow strip that separates two sashes on a typical double-hung window.

HOW TO TUNE UP DOUBLE-HUNG WINDOWS

1 Loosen a stuck window sash by forcing a putty knife between the sash and the window stop or parting strip. If hand pressure isn't enough to push in the blade, tap the handle with a hammer. Loosen both sides of the sash.

2 Once the sash is free, push it out of the way and clean out any debris from the sash channel using an old chisel or stiff, narrow putty knife.

3 Clean up the channel by sanding all three surfaces smooth. Use 100-grit paper wrapped around a scrap block of wood. Brush away the sanding dust or vacuum it up.

TIP:

Sashes that bind only slightly can often be freed by tapping the stop with a small block of wood. Don't strike the block too hard. This could split the stop. Firm taps should do the trick.

4 Paraffin is a good lubricant for sash channels. Just rub a candle vigorously against all three surfaces of both channels.

5 To remove a bottom sash, take off the stop trim on both jambs that hold the sash in place. Slide a chisel or putty knife between the two surfaces and pry gently to avoid splitting the stop.

6 Once the stops are removed the sash can swing free. Remove the weight cords from the sides and cut or plane the sash so it fits the channels better.

7 To free the upper sash, remove the parting strip on both jambs. Grip each strip at the bottom or top with pliers and pull. The parting strips are held only by friction, no fasteners are used. Protect the strip with small scrap blocks on both sides.

7

Repairing Fascia & Soffits

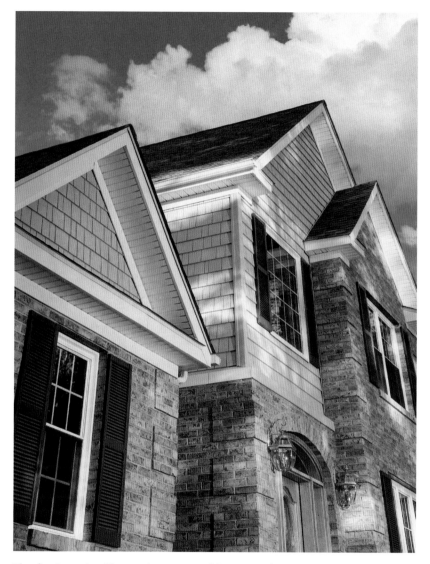

The fascia and soffit are the most visible parts of your roof system.
Keeping them well maintained is very important to the appearance of your
home (and they help keep pests out, too).

FASCIA AND SOFFITS ADD A FINISHED LOOK TO YOUR ROOF AND PROMOTE A
HEALTHY ROOF SYSTEM. A well-ventilated soffit system prevents moisture from building
up under the roof and in the attic.

Most fascia and soffit problems can be corrected by cutting out sections of damaged material and replacing them. Joints between fascia boards are lock-nailed at rafter locations, so you should remove whole sections of fascia to make accurate bevel cuts for patches. Soffits can often be left in place for repairs.

FASCIA & SOFFIT 101

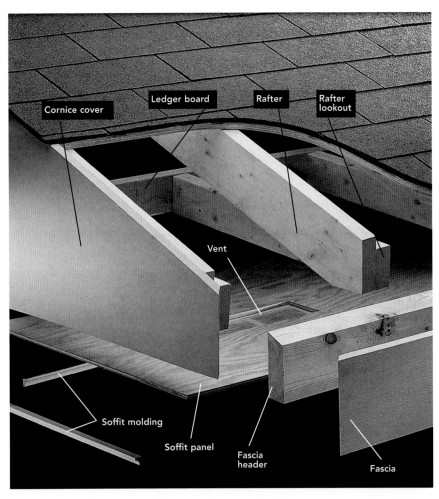

Cornice cover | Ledger board | Rafter | Rafter lookout

Vent

Soffit molding

Soffit panel

Fascia header

Fascia

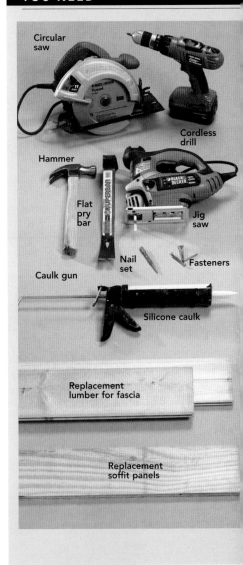

Circular saw

Cordless drill

Hammer

Flat pry bar

Jig saw

Nail set

Fasteners

Caulk gun

Silicone caulk

Replacement lumber for fascia

Replacement soffit panels

Fascia and soffits close off the eaves area beneath the roof overhang. The fascia covers the ends of rafters and rafter lookouts, and provides a surface for attaching gutters. Soffits are protective panels that span the area between the fascia and the side of the house.

TERMS YOU NEED TO KNOW

FASCIA—Horizontal trim boards that conceal the rafter ends in the eave area of a house.

SOFFITS—Panels that close in the underside of the eave area, usually spanning from the fascia to the exterior wall. They can be made of sheet goods (¼" plywood), tongue-and-groove boards or vinyl, steel or aluminum to match your siding.

DIFFICULTY LEVEL

SKILLS LEVEL

EASY   MODERATE

Actual project time varies according to amount of damage and type of material.

HOW TO REPAIR WOOD PANEL SOFFITS

TIP: Cut soffits as close as possible to the rafters or rafter lookouts. Finish cuts with a chisel, if necessary.

1 In the area where soffits are damaged, remove the support moldings that hold the soffits in place along the fascia and exterior wall. Drill entry holes, then use a jig saw to cut out the damaged soffit area.

2 Remove the damaged soffit section, using a pry bar. Cut nailing strips the same length as the exposed area of the rafters, and fasten them to the rafters or rafter lookouts at the edges of the openings, using 2½" deck screws.

3 Using soffit material similar to the original panel, cut a replacement piece ⅛" smaller than the opening. If the new panel will be vented, cut the vent openings.

4 Attach the replacement panel to the nailing strips, using 2" deck screws. If you are not going to paint the entire soffit after the repair, prime and paint the replacement piece before installing it.

5 Reattach the soffit molding, using 4d galvanized casing nails. Set nail heads with a nail set.

6 Using paintable exterior caulk, fill all nail holes, screw holes, and gaps. Smooth out the caulk with a putty knife until the caulk is even with the surface. Prime and paint the soffit panels.

HOW TO REPAIR WOOD FASCIA

1 Remove gutters, shingle moldings, and other items mounted on the fascia. Pry off the damaged board with a pry bar. Remove the entire board and all old nails. If there is no fascia backer board, mark the end of the nearest rafter to the damage for cutting.

2 Set your circular saw to cut a 45 degree bevel, and cut off the damaged portion of the fascia board so the cutline will be centered on a rafter end. Reattach the undamaged portion of the fascia. Cut a patch board, making a bevel cut that's opposite to the trim cut.

3 Set the patch board in place. Drill pilot holes through both fascia boards into the rafter. Replace shingle moldings and trim pieces, using 4d galvanized casing nails. Set the nail heads. Prime and paint the new board.

8

Exterior Caulking

Caulk guns are used to deliver a wide range of household products, not simply caulk. The guns are tricky to use at first, but with practice you'll get the hang of it.

WHEN YOU VISIT EVEN A MODEST HARDWARE STORE YOU WILL BE CONFRONT-ED WITH AT LEAST TEN DIFFERENT KINDS OF CAULK, ALL IN THE SAME-SIZE TUBES. It is possible, naturally, to read the labels and find out what the manufacturer says the caulk should do. But who wants to spend that kind of time and effort on cheap goop?

Well, maybe you should, if you want to save money on heating and air-conditioning costs, keep insects out, and prevent water from working its way behind your siding. Caulk can do all of this and more. You just have to buy a couple of tubes, spring for a caulk gun (about $4), and spend a little time filling house holes.

Any holes cut through the outside envelope of the house for services, like electricity, telephone, cable or satellite dishes, gas pipes, clothes dryer vents, outdoor receptacles and light fixtures, and garden hose sillcocks are candidates for caulking. Then hunt down the cracks that open up between the siding boards and the trim boards, like the window and door casings, the corner boards and baseboard trim along the bottom of the walls.

CAULK 101

Among the many products available for purchase in caulk-style cartridges are true caulks (usually made of silicone, acrylic, latex or a combination), but you'll also find specialty products that are formulated for specific materials, such as concrete. Some manufacturers list longevity ratings, which should really only be used for comparison purposes among similar brands.

TERMS YOU NEED TO KNOW

SILICONE ACRYLIC CAULK—A resilient gap-filling compound made with acrylic and silicone resins that's very flexible, durable, and has a low coefficient of thermal expansion. Cleans up with soap and water.

Exterior primer and paint

Caulk gun

Silicone acrylic caulk

Old paint-brush

Utility knife

Putty knife

DIFFICULTY LEVEL

SKILLS LEVEL

EASY   MODERATE

This project can be completed in one to six hours.

1 Exterior light fixtures rarely fit tightly to the siding. To block the air infiltration, apply a bead of caulk all the way around the base. Smooth the bead with a wet finger.

3 Dryer vent hoods occupy a lot of area and a loose one lets in a lot of air. If the hood rests on beveled siding, there may be large voids where the siding boards lap. Fill these holes with caulk and smooth the bead with your finger.

2 Exterior receptacles have a gasket between the cover plate and the box. However, nothing blocks the air movement around the box. Caulk around the box to fill these holes.

BUYING CAULK

Wading through the variety of caulks available is imposing but, fortunately, not impossible. For exterior use you want something flexible and durable, and the best choice is a silicone acrylic caulk. These products are more expensive than basic acrylic latex caulk but they perform better. They also clean up with water, which is a real plus. Sometimes this caulk is available in colors but usually you'll find it only in clear and white versions. If you need color, you'll have to paint over the caulk after it's dry—but make sure you buy paintable caulk.

APPLYING CAULK

Using caulk is messy, especially if you over-fill holes and then try to wipe off the excess. Cut the tip off the tube applicator to match the size of most of the holes you want to fill. Use a sharp utility knife and angle the cut to about 45 degrees to get the best bead. Poke the inside membrane of the tube by pushing a long nail down through the applicator. Then slide the tube into the gun, click the trigger a few times so the plunger bears against the bottom of the tube and squeeze the handle. As the caulk starts flowing, move the tip along the hole or crack until it's full.

4 Old caulk that is cracked or pulling away from the joint should be removed. Cut both sides of the old caulk using a carpet knife or utility knife and pull the debris from the joint. Remove dust with an old paintbrush.

5 Once the caulk is removed, prime the crack with exterior primer. Make sure to coat all the exposed wood.

6 After the primer dries, caulk the joint and smooth the bead with your finger or a putty knife.

7 Finish up the job by brushing on two coats of paint. Allow the caulk to dry, according to the manufacturer's instructions, before you paint.

Pressure Washing
a House

9

Pressure washers can be rented or you can buy your own light-duty model for around $100.
Washing your siding is just one of the many useful chores a pressure washer can perform.

SELF-SERVICE CAR WASHES ARE A GREAT IDEA. THEY LET YOU WASH YOUR CAR THE WAY YOU WANT TO WASH IT, AND THEY LEAVE YOU ALONE. If you could fit your house into a self-serve car wash, you might never need a pressure washer of your own. That is, until you think a little. What about washing the car at home, getting off the caked-on grass from the bottom of the mower, blowing away the stains on the garage floor, banishing the dirt from your backyard deck, and prevailing over the mildew on all that plastic outdoor furniture? A pressure washer makes all these jobs easier and quicker than other approaches. And, it does a wonderful job of washing your house.

PRESSURE WASHERS 101

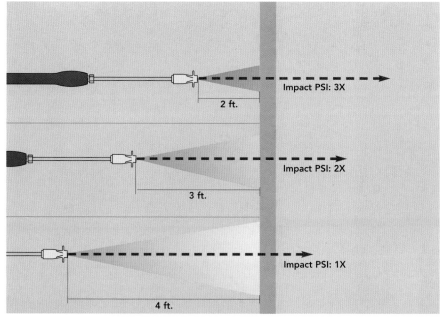

Impact PSI: 3X
2 ft.

Impact PSI: 2X
3 ft.

Impact PSI: 1X
4 ft.

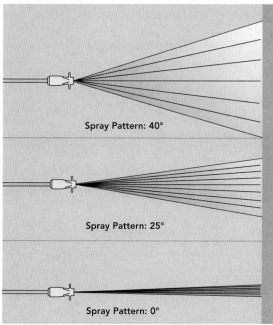

Spray Pattern: 40°

Spray Pattern: 25°

Spray Pattern: 0°

There are two ways to adjust cleaning power using the pressure washer. You can adjust the distance (above) that you hold the nozzle from the surface you are cleaning. The second way is to change the spray pattern (left). Some pressure washers also allow you to adust the pressure regulator knob on the engine or water pump. This enables you to fine-tune the water pressure without altering the distance or spray pattern.

BUYING A PRESSURE WASHER

You can find a very good pressure washer for as little as $100, but it won't be a 3000 psi machine that you could use to spruce up the Sears Tower. Instead, it will be an electric model that delivers about 1500 psi and about 2 gallons per minute (gpm) of flow. Multiplying the pressure (psi) and water flow (gpm) ratings yields a rating a figure called the cleaning power (CP) for each model. A machine with a CP rating of 3000 will do everything you want around the house without the risk of injury from puncture wounds that are possible with the higher pressure machines.

Pressure washer with detergent siphon tube

Bleach

Degreaser solution

Liquid detergent

Rotating scrub brush

Plastic sheeting

Rubber gloves

Detergent siphon tube

Scrub brush

DIFFICULTY LEVEL

SKILLS LEVEL

EASY   MODERATE

This project can be completed in one to three days.

HOW TO PRESSURE WASH A HOUSE

1 If using detergents, cover the plants around your house with tarps or plastic sheeting. Leave the cover on only when you are working. If it stays on for long periods during hot weather, the plants can die from exposure to too much heat.

2 You have the option to add cleaning detergent to the machine's water flow by installing a standard siphon tube between the machine and a container of detergent.

3 If the siding is very dirty, you may have to use a rotating scrub brush accessory to clean the surface. The brush can use either clean water or dispense a soapy solution. This is a bit like pre-cleaning stains on clothing before laundering.

TIP FOR REMOVING STAINS

Stubborn mildew and rust stains usually need hand scrubbing with a weak bleach solution. Use a sponge or brush to clean the area and rinse the area thoroughly. Be sure to wear protective gloves.

4 To prevent streaks on house siding, start pressure washing on the bottom and work up. Use the same approach whether you're using plain water or soapy water.

5 To rinse the side, start at the top and work down. The clean water will flush away any dirt and soap residue and leave behind a clean surface.

CLEANING OTHER OUTDOOR SURFACES

A pressure washer also works on surfaces like wood decks. Sometimes a quick spraying with plain water will do the trick. But more typically, the deck has to be cleaned chemically and then rinsed with plain water.

Concrete steps, walks and driveways respond very well to pressure washing. Because the spray tip can be held so close to the surface without causing any damage, usually water alone will do the trick. But oil stains on a garage floor will require a detergent wash and possibly a prewash with a degreaser solution.

10

Fixing A Concrete Walk

Once a concrete sidewalk or driveway starts to fail, you can bet it that it's just the beginning of the problem. By fixing the crack or chip-out right away you can preserve the concrete.

CONCRETE CERTAINLY HAS AN ATTITUDE. It's hard, stubborn, and uncompromising; it won't bend even when a little give-and-take would make everything easier. Fortunately, it's more than just tough. It's also durable, long lasting, and faithful.

Everybody thinks concrete is so tough that they can do anything to it and it will be fine. Up to a point this is true. There isn't too much that puny humans can do, in the normal course of life, to cause any real damage. But the weather is something else, especially the kind of weather that gets below freezing in the winter. The freeze and thaw cycle creates little cracks that soon become bigger cracks as water seeps in, freezes and expands. If repairs aren't made when the problems are small, the problems will never be small again.

CONCRETE CRACKS 101

Cracks in concrete typically must be made worse before they are made better. By chiseling the top of the crack so the walls slope down and away from the crack, you create a bell shape that will hold the repair material in place. You can fill cracks up to about ½" in. wide × ½" deep with a liquid polymer crack filler available at lumberyards and home centers. Fill the cracks just slightly below the surrounding surface for the best appearance. Then cover the cracks for two days so they aren't damaged by foot traffic. Deeper cracks should first be filled to within ½" of the top with foam backer rods. These should be compressed in the crack with a screwdriver or a putty knife and then covered with crack filler. If the crack is over ½" wide, fill the gap in a couple of applications so everything has time to cure properly. Breaks along the edge of the walk are the hardest to repair, but with a little effort, you can help that walk maintain its edge just a bit longer.

TERMS YOU NEED TO KNOW

FOAM BACKER RODS—Tube-shaped sections of foam for filling wide holes before caulking is applied. Commonly available in various lengths and in diameters from ¼" up to 2 in.

SPALLED CONCRETE—Concrete surface damage that appears as a flaking away of the top layer, usually less than 1/16" deep.

TOOLS & SUPPLIES YOU NEED

DIFFICULTY LEVEL

This project can be completed in one to two hours per four foot square section of sidewalk.

HOW TO FIX A CONCRETE CHIP-OUT

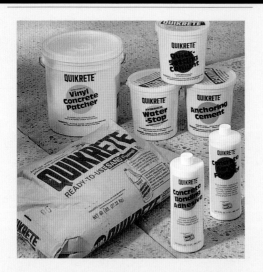

CONCRETE PATCHING materials contain additives and reinforcement to accomplish specific tasks. Shop carefully at your building center to make sure you buy the best product for your repair.

1 Drive a form board next to the sidewalk and undercut the broken section with a cold chisel and hammer. This will create a modest keyway that will give the patch something extra to grip.

2 Just prior to applying the patch, brush some clean water onto the broken area to help the patch bond better.

3 Use a small mortar trowel to apply the mortar patch. Be sure to force the patch to the bottom of the hole and feather the edges so the patch blends in well with the surrounding surfaces.

4 To reduce the chance of the edge breaking again, round it off using an edging tool. Gently move the tool over the patch and try to match the edge troweling on the rest of the walk.

5 Lightly brush the surface of the patch with a stiff broom. This creates better traction for bad weather conditions. When you're done, cover the patch with a plastic trap for 6 or 7 days.

HOW TO FIX A CONCRETE CRACK

1 Remove any dust and debris from cracks with a wire brush, vacuum cleaner or a compressor with a hose-mounted spray nozzle.

2 Squeeze crack filler in the crack, stopping just below the surface of the walk. This protects the cracks without running the risk of smearing the filler across the surrounding surfaces.

Repairing An Asphalt Driveway

11

Asphalt is a relatively forgiving paving material. When popouts or cracks occur, repairing them is basically a matter of dumping in fresh material and picking a way to compress it.

THE TWO MOST POPULAR HARD SURFACE DRIVEWAY MATERIALS ARE ASPHALT AND CONCRETE. Both are used, almost interchangeably, throughout the country in cold and hot climates. But there are some basic differences. Concrete generally costs more to install and asphalt generally costs more to maintain as the years go by. And, concrete doesn't always perform well in cold areas. It's susceptible to damage from the freeze-and-thaw cycle and it can be damaged by exposure to road salt. Asphalt, on the other hand, doesn't always perform well in hot climates. It absorbs a lot of heat from the sun and tends to stay soft during very hot periods. And, of course, when the surface is soft, it can wear more quickly.

It's a good thing that concrete doesn't need much routine maintenance because doing just about anything to concrete is difficult. Asphalt, however, is very easy to maintain and repair. And there are plenty of products in local home centers to help anyone do the work. In many ways, fixing an asphalt driveway is a lot like repainting a house that is in bad shape. Most of the work deals with surface preparation. Applying a new coat of driveway sealer is only the last of many steps.

DRIVEWAY SEALER 101

TOOLS & SUPPLIES YOU NEED

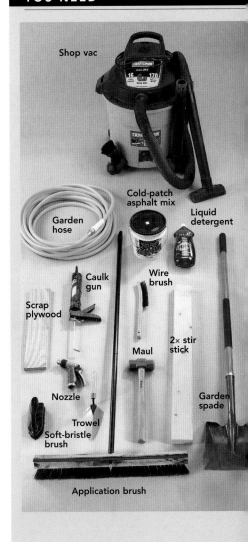

Shop vac

Cold-patch asphalt mix

Liquid detergent

Garden hose

Caulk gun

Wire brush

Scrap plywood

2× stir stick

Maul

Nozzle

Garden spade

Trowel

Soft-bristle brush

Application brush

Some driveway sealers are made of coal tar, others are asphalt emulsions. Coal tar is compatible with asphalt paving and has some durability advantages over asphalt because it has ultra-violet stabilizers in the mix. These keep the black color of the sealer from fading quickly. Coal tar also resists damage from gas and oil spills better than asphalt. Both types are sold in 5 gal. buckets that sell for about $20 and cover between 300 and 400 sq. ft. of surface area.

The trick with applying sealers is to do it in warm weather (nothing below 50 degrees F.). Also, you should apply the sealer in thinner, rather than thicker, coats. If you build up too thick a coat, the sealer can peel. The container directions on the product you buy will indicate the proper coverage rate.

TERMS YOU NEED TO KNOW

ASPHALT—A combination of bitumens—that are by-products of coal tar distillation—and aggregates—that are a mixture of sand and gravel. Installed when hot.

ASPHALT SEALER—A bituminous coating, sometimes including sand as a fine aggregate, that is used to seal the surface of asphalt pavement.

ASPHALT—A paste-like combination of bitumens, very fine aggregate and additives to keep the mixture malleable.

ASPHALT CRACK FILLER—Comes in different formulations. One is a rubberized liquid emulsion that stays flexible permanently.

COLD-PATCH ASPHALT MIX—A combination of asphalt and synthetic polymers that keep the asphalt workable when it's cool.

DIFFICULTY LEVEL

SKILLS LEVEL

EASY   MODERATE

This project can be completed in eight to twelve hours.

HOW TO REPAIR AN ASPHALT DRIVEWAY

X-SECTION OF ASPHALT DRIVEWAY

Asphalt layer

Subbase

Soil

A typical asphalt driveway is formed by pouring and compressing a layer of hot asphalt over a subbase of compacted gravel.

1 Begin the maintenance routine by removing any grass, weeds and other vegetation from the surface and sides of the driveway. Use a long-handle ice scraper or a square-tip shovel.

2 Carefully inspect the asphalt surface for any oil and grease stains. Then remove them with driveway cleaner or household detergent. Scrub the cleaner into the surface with a soft brush and rinse the area clean with a garden hose. Repeat until the stain is gone. If using driveway cleaner, wear the recommended safety equipment.

3 Once the stains are removed, thoroughly rinse the entire driveway with a garden hose and nozzle. The goal is to wash away any debris and to remove the dust and dirt from the surface cracks.

4 Repair the small cracks first. Chip out any loose debris with a cold chisel and hammer. Then clean out all debris with a wire brush. Remove all the dust with a shop vacuum. A crevice tool on the end of the hose will do the best job.

5 Place asphalt patching compound in the holes with a small trowel. Overfill the hole so the patch material is about ½" higher than the surrounding asphalt surface.

6 Compact the patch material with a small piece of 2 × 4. Tamp the board up and down with your hand, or strike the board with a hammer. Keep working until you can't compress the patch any more.

7 Finish the patch by covering it with a piece of 2 × 6 and striking it with a hammer or mallet. Work back and forth across the board to smooth out the entire patch and make it flush to the surrounding surface.

8 On narrower patches, the compound can be smoothed with a small trowel. Just move the tool across the surrounding surface and then over the patch. This should flatten the patch. Finish up by compressing the compound by pushing it down with the trowel.

9 Prepare larger potholes by undercutting the edges with a cold chisel and a hammer. Then, remove all the debris and fill the hole with cold-patch asphalt mix. Working directly from the bag, fill the hole about 1 in. higher than the surrounding surface. Then compact it with a 2×4, as before.

10 One great way to compress cold-patch asphalt is to cover the patch with a piece of plywood. Then, drive your car onto the plywood and stop when one tire is centered on the panel. Wait a few minutes, then move the car back and forth a few times.

11 Once the hole patching is done, fill the routine cracks (less than ¼" wide) with asphalt crack filler. This material comes in a caulk tube, which makes it very easy to apply. Just clean the crack with a wire brush and a vacuum, then squeeze the filler into the crack.

12 After the crack filler has cured for about 10 or 15 minutes, smooth it out with a putty knife as you force the filler down into the crack. If this creates small depressions, fill these with a second application of filler.

13 Driveway sealer should always be mixed thoroughly before use. Take a 2× stir stick that's about 30 in. long and stir the sealer until it has a uniform consistency. Pour out enough to cover a strip across the driveway that's about 3-ft. or 4-ft. wide.

14 Spread the sealer with the squeegee side of the application brush. Try to keep this coat as uniform as possible. Work the sealer into the small cracks and pull it gently over the big patches.

15 Flip the squeegee over to the brush side and smooth out the lap marks and other irregularities that were left from the application coat. Work at right angles to the first pass.

Fixing Broken
Glass Panes

12

Replacing a broken glass pane isn't nearly as common an occurrence today as it was a decade or two ago. But it's still a great skill to have for owners of older homes.

FOR PEOPLE WHO LIVE IN NEW, WELL-MADE HOUSES THE WINDOWS FROM THE GROUND TO THE RIDGE ARE BOUND TO BE DOUBLE-GLAZED UNITS THAT PER-FORM WITH COMMENDABLE ENERGY EFFICIENCY. This is a good thing, mostly. But these hi-tech units can break just like their older single-pane siblings, and you just can't fix double-glazed sashes yourself. People who live in older houses have it better. Their single pane sashes and storm windows are easy and inexpensive to repair. If you have just one pane to replace, most people can finish up the job in a couple of hours. Usually the hardest part of this chore is working off a ladder. You'll need one to remove the storm windows and to fix a regular sash because the repair needs to be made on the outside of the window.

GLASS PANES 101

Each glass pane in a typical wood sash is held in place on the inside by the wood that forms the sash and on the outside by glazing compound. This compound is a soft, caulk-like material when it's installed. But it hardens over time to form a durable seal that keeps the glass in the frame and the water out. If you wiggle the pieces of broken glass in-and-out, this will loosen the compound and you can pull the shards out. Measure the space, go to the hardware store for a $2 piece of glass, pop it in and glaze.

TERMS YOU NEED TO KNOW

WINDOW SASH—Any framework that holds window glazing, as in a double-hung window with two sashes (that is, two wood frames that each hold one or multiple pieces of glass).

GLAZIER'S POINTS—Small triangular pieces of steel with one side bent up at a 90-degree angle. Made for holding glass panes within wood frames, these points are pushed into place with a putty knife or flat blade screwdriver.

HOW TO FIX A BROKEN WINDOW PANE

1 Wearing heavy leather gloves, remove the broken pieces of glass. Then, soften the old glazing compound using a heat gun or a hair dryer. Don't hold the heat gun too long in one place because it can be hot enough to scorch the wood.

2 Once a section of compound is soft, remove it using a putty knife. Work carefully to avoid gouging the wood frame. If a section is difficult to scrape clean, reheat it with the heat gun. Soft compound is always easy to remove.

3 Once the wood opening is scraped clean, seal the wood with a coat of linseed oil or primer. If the wood isn't sealed, the dry surface will draw too much moisture from the glazing compound and reduce its effectiveness.

4 Apply a thin bed of glazing compound to the wood frame opening and smooth it in place with your thumb.

5 Press the new pane into the opening, making sure to achieve a tight seal with the compound on all sides. Wiggle the pane from side-to-side and up-and-down until the pane is seated. There will be some squeeze-out, but do not press all the compound out.

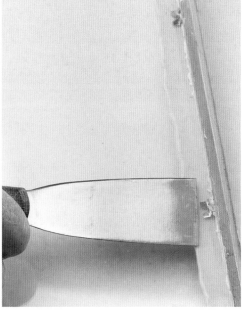

6 Drive glazier's points into the wood frame to hold the pane in place. Use the tip of a putty knife to slide the point against the surface of the glass. Install at least 2 points of each side of the pane.

7 Make a rope of compound (about ½" diameter) by rolling it between your hands. Then press it against the pane and the wood frame. Smooth it in place by drawing a putty knife, held at a 45-degree angle, across its surface. Scrape off excess.

8 Allow the glazing compound at least one week to dry completely. Then prime and paint it to match the rest of the sash. Be sure to spread the paint over the joint between the compound and the glass. This will seal the joint completely. When the paint is dry, scrape off the extra with a razor blade paint scraper.

13

Repairing Concrete Steps

A little concrete patching material and some know-how will keep your concrete steps looking brand new.

BUILDERS USE A LOT OF DIFFERENT MATERIALS FOR ENTRY STEPS. Many familiar varieties of stone and brick are common choices. Wood is also a favorite, especially for rustic buildings or those that are blessed with a large front porch. But when you look at all the houses and all the entry doors, including those at the back and side of the house, concrete has to be the top choice, by far. That's because it's cheap, durable, and long lasting.

The biggest problem involved in making a successful concrete step repair is binding the patch material to the existing material. Strong bonds can be created with the use of a bonding agent, usually part of the patching mix. The second bonding problem is that the repair surface must be free of all dust, dirt, grease and debris. Unless it is thoroughly cleaned, the patch won't hold for long.

CONCRETE CRACK REPAIR 101

Small cracks (about ¼ in. wide and deep) can be filled with concrete crack filler. Just brush out the crack and squeeze in the filler, stopping just a bit below the top of the crack. For wider cracks, one good approach is to fill the crack with mortar. Breaks along the edges and corners are repaired with a form board (or boards) nailed to the side of the steps. Then the edges of the break are under-cut with a cold chisel and the void filled with a concrete patch mix. For big breaks, it's a good idea to drive masonry nails into the middle of the void to act as reinforcement for the patch. Make sure to drive these nails deep enough so their heads won't sit above the finished surface.

Mortar patch mix

Bonding agent

Steel float

Circular saw with masonry blade

Edging tool

Pointing trowel

Paintbrush

Cold chisel

Wire brush

Plastic sheeting

Form boards

DIFFICULTY LEVEL

SKILLS LEVEL

EASY   MODERATE

This project can be completed in two to five hours.

TERMS YOU NEED TO KNOW

CONCRETE CRACK FILLER—A liquid polymer substance that dries into a flexible, watertight seal.

BONDING AGENT—An adhesive chemical substance that's applied between a concrete substrate and a mortar patching mix.

MORTAR PATCHING MIX—A mixture of cement, sand, water and admixtures like bonding agents and plasticizers to make the material more workable.

HOW TO REPAIR BROKEN CONCRETE

1 Retrieve the broken corner, then clean it and the mating surface with a wire brush. Apply latex bonding agent to both surfaces. If you do not have the broken piece, you can rebuild the corner with patching compound.

2 Spread a heavy layer of fortified patching compound on the surfaces to be joined, then press the broken piece into position. Lean a heavy brick or block against the repair until the patching compound sets (about 30 minutes). Cover the repair with plastic and protect it from traffic for at least one week.

HOW TO REBUILD WITH PATCHING COMPOUND

1 Clean chipped concrete with a wire brush. Brush the patch area with latex bonding agent.

2 Mix patching compound with latex bonding agent, as directed by the manufacturer. Apply the mixture to the patch area, then smooth the surfaces and round the edges, as necessary, using a flexible knife or trowel.

3 Tape scrap lumber pieces around the patch as a form. Coat the insides with vegetable oil or commercial release agent so the patch won't adhere to the wood. Remove the wood when the patch is firm. Cover with plastic and protect from traffic for at least one week.

HOW TO REBUILD A BROKEN STEP

1 Make a cut in the stair tread just outside the damaged area, using a circular saw with a masonry-cutting blade. Make the cut so it angles toward the back of the step. Make a horizontal cut on the riser below the damaged area, then chisel out the area in between the two cuts.

2 Cut a form board the same height as the step riser. Coat one side of the board with vegetable oil or commercial release agent to prevent it from bonding with the repair, then press it against the riser of the damaged step, and brace it in position with heavy blocks. Make sure the top of the form is flush with the top of the step tread.

3 Apply latex bonding agent to the repair area with a clean paint brush, wait until the bonding agent is tacky (no more than 30 minutes), then press a stiff mixture of quick-setting cement into the damaged area with a trowel.

4 Smooth the concrete with a float, and let it set for a few minutes. Round over the front edge of the nose with an edger. Use a trowel to slice off the sides of the patch, so it is flush with the side of the steps. Cover the repair with plastic and wait a week before allowing traffic on the repaired section.

Repairing And Painting A Fence

14

Fence damage often looks worse than it is. You could undertake a back-breaking demolition and rebuild to deal with a rotted post...but there is an easier way.

MOST WOOD FENCES ARE PRETTY SIMPLE. Unfortunately, the bad effects of exposure to the elements take their toll on wood fences. Posts will rot out where they meet the ground, as will bottom rails that sometimes sit in snow for long periods and are splashed with rain water the rest of the year. Older fences also have a tendency to lean one way or the other, usually as a result of frost movement in the ground. And no matter how good the structural condition of your fence, if it's been painted once it will need painting again, and again for the rest of its life. Here's how to deal with all these problems.

You can replace rotted posts, but it's a lot of work and it's not really necessary. After all, the problem with the post is where it meets the ground. The part that holds the rails and boards is usually fine. So, it makes better sense to reinforce the bottom of the post with a stub post installed right next to it.

Sometimes fence rails are just loose and they can be tightened by replacing the fasteners that hold them to the posts. Galvanized nails or screws are good for this job. If replacing the fasteners doesn't stiffen the rail enough, add galvanized T-brackets to the joint to provide extra support. But sometimes a rail is so rotted that it has to be replaced. This job can be a pain but if approached methodically should take only an hour or two.

WOOD FENCES 101

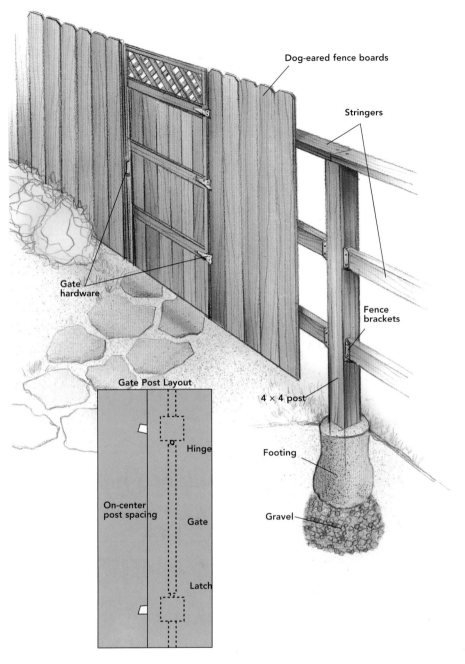

Dog-eared fence boards

Stringers

Gate hardware

Gate Post Layout

Hinge

On-center post spacing

Gate

Latch

4 × 4 post

Fence brackets

Footing

Gravel

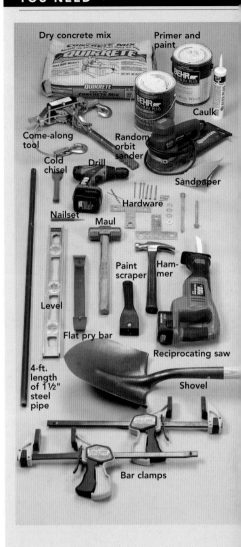

Dry concrete mix

Primer and paint

Caulk

Come-along tool

Random orbit sander

Cold chisel

Drill

Sandpaper

Hardware

Nailset

Maul

Paint scraper

Ham-mer

Level

Flat pry bar

Reciprocating saw

4-ft. length of 1½" steel pipe

Shovel

Bar clamps

Fences are pretty simple. They consist of vertical posts that are embedded in the ground and hold the whole structure up, horizontal rails that tie the posts together and provide nailing surfaces for the fence boards, and the fence boards that fill the space between posts and give the structure its character.

DIFFICULTY LEVEL

SKILLS LEVEL

EASY   MODERATE

This project can be completed in two to three days depending on the problems.

TERMS YOU NEED TO KNOW

COME-ALONG TOOL—A hand-operated winch, typically with a steel hook on one end and a cable-mounted steel hook on the other. Made to allow one person to move heavy loads, or to tighten shipping straps.

HOW TO REPAIR & PAINT A FENCE

1 To repair a rotted post, first break up the concrete collar (if the post has one) and cut off the rotted section at the bottom of the post with a hand saw or reciprocating saw. Then dig out the cut section of the old post and collar with a shovel.

2 Brace the fence to compensate for the cut post, then cut a stub post to length and put it in the hole next to the old post. Plumb it and brace it in the plumb position. Then fill around the stub with concrete.

3 Make sure the fence rails are level and the fence boards are vertical. Drill countersunk guide holes all the way through the stub post, the old post and the fence rails and fence boards. Tap a carriage bolt into each hole. Add and tighten washers and nuts.

4 Tighten a loose rail by replacing its fasteners with galvanized nails or screws. Be sure to set the nail heads below the surface with a nailset.

5 To improve the strength of a rail-to-post joint, install a galvanized T-bracket with galvanized or stainless steel screws.

6 To replace a rotted rail, first remove the fasteners from the face of the fence boards. If screws were used just back them out with a cordless drill. But if you find nails, the fence boards have to be pried away from the rail with a flat pry bar. Once the nails are loose, pull them with a hammer or nail puller.

7 Cut a new rail to length and slide it between the posts. Support the rail on a block of wood clamped to the post on both ends.

8 Attach the new rail to the posts by driving angled galvanized screws through the rail and into the post. Once the rails are stable, screw the fence boards to the rail.

HOW TO REPAIR & PAINT A FENCE

9 To fix a leaning fence, first dig around the base of all the leaning posts to free them for movement. Then push against the fence with several friends until it is plumb. When it is, brace it in place.

10 If you are working alone, you can straighten the fence using a come-along tool. To use it, first drive a screw eye near the top of any leaning post.

11 Next drive a length of steel pipe into the ground, at a 45 degree angle, about 5 feet from the post. Hook the come-along to the screw eye and the pipe and start ratcheting the come-along. This will pull over the top of the fence until it's plumb. Brace the first post and move on to others that are leaning.

12 Once all the posts have been pulled straight, recheck everything for plumb, then fill around the bottoms of the posts with concrete. Wait at least three days for the concrete to dry, then remove the braces.

13 To paint a fence, begin by scraping off any flaking paint with a paint scraper. If you find any loose fasteners, re-drive them or replace them.

14 Sand the scraped paint to smooth the edges, using an electric sander and 80- or 100-grit paper. For most jobs a random orbit sander works best. These tools are easy to control and they sand faster than a regular finishing sander.

15 Thoroughly prime all the fence parts with exterior primer. Once the surface is dry, fill any holes and cracks with paintable exterior caulk.

16 Paint the fence with two top coats of oil-base or 100-percent acrylic paint. Wait a day between coats.

Fixing A Worn Gate

15

A gate that has structural damage, a failed hinge or a gate post that's out of plumb will cease to perform its primary function. In this chapter we'll walk you through several easy gate repairs.

THESE DAYS THE TERM PORTAL SOUNDS PRETTY SERIOUS. That's because it's most frequently used in the context of an Internet portal. And, as we all know, the Internet is a very serious thing. As a matter of fact, just about everything associated with the digital cosmos demands and assumes respect. Living in this brave new world must be very satisfying. But for those of us who are too old or too diffident to assimilate, portal has a more prosaic meaning: a doorway or gate. And there's not much nuance in either idea. Both are simple swinging devices, usually made of wood, that provide a useful break in a wall or a fence. Doors may run things on the inside of a house, but outside is where gates take over.

Generally speaking, a gate is only as good as how much it's been used. The weight of a gate, especially a wet one, is a real strain on the hinges and on the fence post that the hinges are mounted on. Just about every problem a gate can have is centered in this joint between the hinges and the post. If you are having trouble with your gate (it's sticking, won't close completely or the latch doesn't work) look here first.

GATES 101

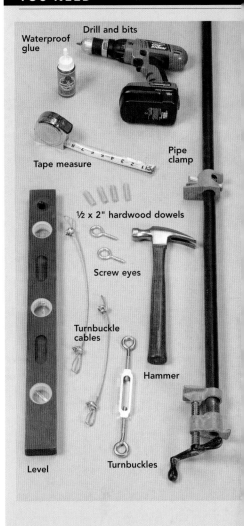

Waterproof glue

Drill and bits

Tape measure

Pipe clamp

½ x 2" hardwood dowels

Screw eyes

Turnbuckle cables

Hammer

Level

Turnbuckles

The most likely parts of a gate system to cause problems are the gate itself, the gate posts and the gate hinges.

HINGES: In many cases the hinge screws come loose. One way to fix this is to move the hinge so the screws can be driven into solid lumber, but an easier approach may be to replace the deteriorated wood in the existing screw holes and re-hang the hinge in the same place it was before.

GATES: If your gate is sticking or won't close completely, it's probably out of square. Instead of rebuilding, remove the gate, place it on a flat surface and coax it back into square with a pipe clamp. Use a turnbuckle to keep the gate square.

POSTS: Fence posts can lean into the opening and pinch the gate so it can't swing freely. You can plane the gate so it fits into the opening better, but a more permanent solution is to stabilize the posts with a turnbuckle and cable.

DIFFICULTY LEVEL

SKILLS LEVEL

EASY   MODERATE

This project can be completed in four to six hours.

TERMS YOU NEED TO KNOW

TURNBUCKLE CABLE—A galvanized hardware fixture that has a right-hand threaded screw eye on one end and a left-hand screw eye on the other, both of which are connected to galvanized steel cables. By turning the turnbuckle the wires are tightened or loosened.

HOW TO FIX A WORN GATE

1 If the hinge screws have loosened, remove the gate and drill ½" diameter holes just under 2" deep in the posts at each hinge screw hole. A spade bit works well for this job.

2 Coat ½" × 2" dowels with exterior-rated glue and drive them into the holes with a hammer. Wipe up any glue squeeze-out with a rag.

3 Brace the gate in the opening and mark the exact location of the hinge screws. Then bore pilot holes and drive the screws flush to the surface of the hinge.

4 If your gate is out of square, use a pipe clamp to force it back into a square shape. Take diagonal measurements of the frame and apply the clamp on the diagonal that has the longer measurement. Tighten the clamp screw until both diagonal measurements are the same.

5 Screw a temporary brace across one corner of the gate. This should keep the gate square when you remove the pipe clamp.

6 Drive screw eyes into top outside and bottom inside corners of the gate. Then install a turnbuckle cable between the two. Tighten the turnbuckle, remove the temporary brace and re-hang the gate.

TIP FOR FIXING A LEANING GATE POST

If your gate post leans, plumb the gate post (check with a level) and hold it in the plumb position with wood braces. Then install a screw eye near the top of the gate post (inset photo) and at the bottom of the next fence post.

Install a turnbuckle cable between the two screw eyes and tighten it. Remove the braces and check the posts for plumb again. If any adjustment is required, tighten or loosen the turnbuckle.

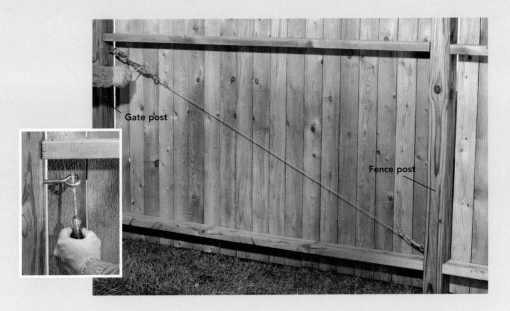

Gate post

Fence post

16

Basic
Siding Repairs

Siding is like the skin of your house and, like the skin on your body, sometimes it gets a scratch or bruise or cut. Here we'll show you how to band-
age the damage.

EXPLAINING HOW TO MAKE BASIC SIDING REPAIRS IS HARDER THAN IT SOUNDS.
That's because there are a lot of different siding types and a lot of variation in the way the
same siding is installed. We show here the repair basics for the most common sidings: clapboard, tongue-and-groove, wood shingles, board-and-batten and vinyl or metal. The chance
that your siding is installed exactly the way you see here is slight, but it's a good place to start.

Clapboard siding is bevel lap siding boards made of redwood or cedar or pine. This siding can
last for well over 100 years, if it's properly maintained.

Tongue-and-groove siding creates a very tight exterior seal and, if the paint and caulk are well
maintained, it is virtually trouble free. But it is difficult and time-consuming to install.

Wood shingles are typically made of cedar or cyprus and may be either split or sawn. This
type of siding may be painted or allowed to weather to a silvery gray.

Vinyl and aluminum siding are designed, installed and repaired in much the same way. Both
products expand and contract a great deal with changes in temperature.

Board-and-batten, in this day and age, normally refers to wood panels (textured plywood)
with thin strips of lumber installed to cover the seams between panels.

EXTERIOR WALLS 101

Wall sheathing

Wall stud

Interior vapor barrier

Siding (clapboard)

Exterior moisture barrier (building paper or house-wrap)

Power miter saw

Trim saw

Caulk guns

Hammer

Zip tool

Keyhole saw or wall-board saw

Flat pry bar

Aviator snips

Fasteners

Mini hacksaw

Hacksaw blade

Siding material for patching

DIFFICULTY LEVEL

SKILLS LEVEL

EASY   MODERATE

This project can be completed in two to three hours, for simple repairs.

Regardless of what type of siding you have, the inside of your exterior walls will look something like this. When you're working on siding, it's important that you identify the locations of wall studs and that you avoid penetrating or tearing the vapor barriers on either side of the wall.

HOW TO REPAIR WOOD CLAPBOARD

1 Locate and mark framing members inside the wall (use a stud finder) so you can draw cutting lines around the damage that fall over studs. Starting at the bottom, cut clapboards at the cutting lines with a keyhole saw or a wallboard saw. For access, slip wood shims under the clapboard above the one you're cutting. NOTE: The repair will look better if you stagger cutting lines so they don't fall on the same stud.

2 Cut replacement clapboards to fit, using a miter saw or power miter saw.

3 Nail the replacement clapboards in the patching area (you can use tape to hold them in place if you like). Follow the same nailing pattern used for the boards around it. Set nail heads with a nailset.

4 Caulk the gaps between clapboards and fill nailholes with exterior putty or caulk. Prime and paint the repaired section to match.

HOW TO REPAIR BOARD & BATTEN

1 With a flat pry bar, remove the battens on each side of the damaged area. To protect the painted surfaces, cut along the joints between the boards and battens with a utility knife before removing the battens.

2 Remove the damaged panel (or make vertical cuts with a circular saw underneath the batten locations if any of the battens are only decorative). Cut a replacement panel from matching material, sized to leave a ⅛" gap between the original panels and the new patch. Nail panel in place, caulk the repair seams and reinstall the battens. Prime and paint to match.

HOW TO REPAIR TONGUE & GROOVE

1 To repair tongue-and-groove siding, first mark both ends of the damage and rip-cut the board down the middle, from end to end, with a circular saw or trim saw. Then use the trim saw to cut along the vertical lines. Finish all cuts with a keyhole saw. Split the damaged board with a pry bar or a wide chisel. Then pull the pieces apart and out of the hole. If the building paper below the damaged section was cut or torn, repair it.

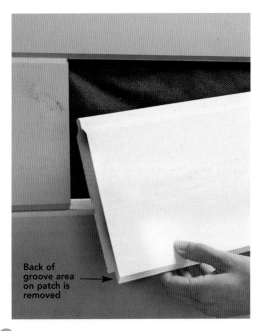

Back of groove area on patch is removed

2 Cut the replacement board to fit, then cut off the backside of the groove so the board can clear the tongue on the course below. Prime the board, let it dry, then nail it into place. Paint to match.

HOW TO REPAIR WOOD SHINGLES

1 Begin repair on a damaged wood shingle by cutting the nails that hold it in place with a mini-hacksaw. Slip shims under the bottom edges of the shingle.

2 Sometimes you can push the shingle in enough to get a grip on the nail head. If so, pull it with a pry bar or a nail puller. Use a small piece of shingle under these tools to avoid splitting adjacent shingles.

3 Take a new shingle and hold it up to the vacant space and mark the width of the opening. Deduct about ⅛" in. for expansion clearance and cut the shingle with a handsaw or a sharp utility knife.

4 Slide the new shingle in place and tap it upward with a hammer until its bottom edge is flush with the shingles next to it. Then nail it in place.

1 Insert a zip tool at the seam nearest the repair area. Slide it over the J-channel, pulling outward slightly, to unlock the joint from the siding below.

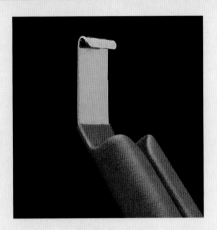

Vinyl and metal siding panels have a locking J-channel that fits over the bottom of the nailing strip on the underlying piece. Use a zip tool to separate panels.

2 Insert spacers between the panels, then remove the fasteners in the damaged siding, using a flat pry bar. Cut out the damaged area, using aviation snips. Cut a replacement piece 4" longer than the open area, and trim 2" off the nailing strip from each end. Slide the piece into position.

3 Insert siding nails in the nailing strip, then position the end of a flat pry bar over each nail head. Drive the nails by tapping on the neck of the pry bar with a hammer. Place a scrap piece of wood between the pry bar and siding to avoid damaging the siding. Slip the locking channel on the overlapping piece over the nailing strip of the replacement piece.

Renewing A
Wood Deck Finish

17

Weathered wood has true romantic appeal, but when the wood is the only thing between your feet and the ground it ought to be in pristine shape. Refinishing a wood deck is vital to that cause (and you'll need to learn how, since you'll be doing it practically every year).

WOOD DECKS CAN BE GREAT THINGS. They give you a place to relax and entertain outside, while maintaining one of the big advantages of staying in: a flat stable floor. In the last 30 years, decks have overtaken the old fashioned patio. One reason for this is that decks are made of wood, not masonry, so the design possibilities are almost limitless. Masonry products, whether concrete, brick, or natural stone, are much harder to work with and are more expensive. Wood decks do wear out and must be maintained to last a long time and look good while doing it.

If you have a small deck (anything under 200 sq. ft.), refinishing is a pretty easy job. But on larger decks, refinishing can develop into quite a chore. The thing to remember, when you've been scrubbing off the old finish for hours, is that replacing a deck can eat up $10,000 nearly as fast as a college bursar. So it pays to take care of things before the deck damage gets out of control.

DECK FINISHING 101

Refinishing a deck involves three separate steps. The first is to remove the old finish. The second is to wash away all the dirt, mildew, and other residues. And the third is to reseal the surface with a new finish. There are lots of products on the market for cleaning decks. The trick is to get the product that's right for your situation. Anything that just says "deck cleaner" is not what's needed. These help lift off dirt and grime but won't do much to remove an old finish. If your deck is covered with just a transparent sealer or a light stain, then a product called a "stain/sealer remover" is what you need. If you have a heavy, solid-color stain, you'll want something stronger. These are sometimes called simply "deck finish strippers," and are made to lift off everything from the surface.

TERMS YOU NEED TO KNOW

DRILL/DRIVER—A cordless drill outfitted with an adjustable clutch that lets the user preset the amount of force used to drive any fastener. Once the drill reaches the preset torque limit, the clutch prevents the chuck from rotating and thus the bit from turning.

LAG SCREWS—A steel screw with a hexagonal head and a thin body with a coarse thread. Used for drawing heavy boards together without using a standard bolt, nut and washers.

CUPPED BOARD—A board that has a convex deviation (a bump) across its width, not its length or thickness.

TOOLS & SUPPLIES YOU NEED

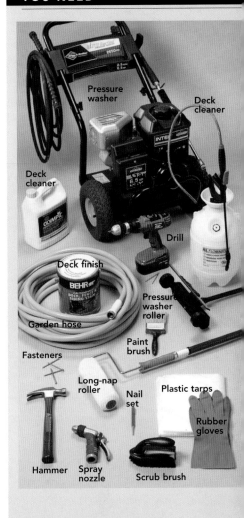

Pressure washer

Deck cleaner

Deck cleaner

Drill

Deck finish

Pressure washer roller

Garden hose

Paint brush

Fasteners

Long-nap roller

Nail set

Plastic tarps

Rubber gloves

Hammer

Spray nozzle

Scrub brush

DIFFICULTY LEVEL

SKILLS LEVEL

EASY   MODERATE

This project can be completed in one to two days depending on size of deck.

HOW TO RENEW A WOOD DECK FINISH

1 Inspect the deck boards, railings and stairs for any loose fasteners. Use lag screws to reinforce stairs and railing posts. Use galvanized or stainless steel screws to tighten down floor boards and balusters.

2 Stair treads are particularly vulnerable to wear. If a step is just wobbly, tighten it with galvanized screws. But if it's split, replace it with a new tread made of pressure treated lumber or composite decking.

3 Nail heads that have lifted from a board can hurt bare feet, and catch shoe heels. Drive them flush with the surface of the board using a hammer and a large nail set.

4 If a floor board is cupped (curved up), try to force it flat against the joist using a galvanized screw. First bore a pilot hole, then drive the screw slowly to avoid splitting the board.

5 Begin refinishing by hosing down the deck and the surrounding area. This will show exactly which areas are worn more than others and will keep debris like dried leaves from blowing on the deck while you work.

6 Use inexpensive plastic tarps to cover any grass, flowers or shrubs that are next to the deck. This will protect them from chemical damage caused by the semi-toxic strippers and cleaners that are used to remove the old finish.

7 Apply a heavy coat of deck stripper to the deck boards. Usually a garden sprayer works for this job. But you can also use a paint roller with a long nap roller to spread the stripper.

8 Let the stripper set for as long as the container directions recommend (usually around 15 minutes). Then brush it vigorously with a stiff bristle deck brush. Try to avoid splattering the stripper on the siding, trim or windows and doors.

9 Hand scrub hard-to-reach spots like built-in benches and railings with a stiff brush. Be sure to wear rubber gloves and eye protection.

10 Rinse off the stripper using a garden hose with a spray attachment or use a pressure washer. Be sure to rinse any adjacent surfaces that might have been splattered with stripper.

11 Next comes the deck cleaner, which is often sold in a concentrated form. Mix it thoroughly in a large bucket, according to the container's directions.

12 Using a stiff deck brush, spread the deck cleaner over the boards and scrub until the wood brightens. Usually, this happens almost immediately. Keep scrubbing until the surface looks new.

13 Once again, rinse the deck with a garden hose or a pressure washer. Also clean the surrounding surfaces and remove the tarps from the shrubs, flowers and lawn. Rinse these plants, but don't get a pressure washer tip too close. Its stream of water will tear the plants apart.

14 Protect surrounding surfaces with masking tape and paper, then start brushing on the sealer. Use the brush just for hard to reach areas. Use a roller on everything else.

15 Keep in mind, when working with the brush, that it tends to hold less sealer than a paint roller. So, to ensure even coverage, load up the brush with extra sealer and apply it in a heavier coat.

16 Apply sealer to the open areas with a roller that has a ¾"-nap roller cover. As you move, press the roller down forcefully so the sealer squeezes between the boards and covers their edges.

Replacing Damaged Roof Shingles

A little bit of localized damage doesn't mean it's time to reroof your whole house. Replacing an old shingle or two can buy you many more years of coverage, but only if the roof doesn't show widespread wear.

THE WORLD OF RESIDENTIAL ROOFING IS PRETTY VARIED. Asphalt, fiberglass-reinforced asphalt, rolled asphalt, wood shingles, wood shakes, slate, concrete, terra cotta tiles, steel, and rubber are just some of the current roofing choices. Why is it with all this choice what you see practically everywhere is asphalt shingles, row after row, all clean-cut, well behaved and just a little bit dull? Well, cost is one thing. Standard three-tab asphalt shingles are priced at about $80 per square (100 square feet of coverage), which is a lot cheaper than other options. Asphalt is also reliable and durable. Twenty-year lifespans are not uncommon.

If you have asphalt shingles on your roof and a small section is damaged, you're in luck. The repair is easy and quick, if only a couple of shingles are involved, so you can do it yourself. There are only two significant obstacles to the job. The first is working from a ladder. If this makes you uncomfortable, hire the job done. The second is that the repair involves a small amount of plastic roof cement. No matter how much you use, this material will get all over you and every tool you touch.

ROOF SAFETY 101

If your roof pitch is 6:12 (6 in. of vertical rise for every 12 in. of horizontal run) or less, then you should be able to work on the roof comfortably and safely. But if your roof is steeper than 6:12, consider getting a contractor. A fall, from even a one-story roof, is a serious matter. To measure a slope, hold a carpenter's square against the roofline, with the top arm horizontal (check it with a level). Position the square so it intersects the roof at the 12" mark. On the vertical arm, measure down from the top to the point of intersection to find the rise.

PROBLEMS YOU'LL NEED TO SOLVE

You can't repair a roof if you don't have some replacement shingles. Fortunately many builders save the shingles that were left over from the original installation. These will be a bit brighter than the ones on the roof that have been faded by the sun. But they'll be close enough. If you don't have any original shingles and can't buy a good match at your local lumberyard, your best strategy is to harvest repair shingles from a less noticeable section of the roof. This means you'll have to repair two roof sections instead of one, but you'll end up with a better looking job.

Caulk gun with roof cement

Flat pry bar or nail puller

Roofing nails

Hammer

Shingles that match the existing roof color

DIFFICULTY LEVEL

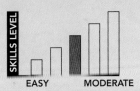

SKILLS LEVEL

EASY   MODERATE

This project can be completed in three to five hours.

HOW TO REPLACE DAMAGED ROOF SHINGLES

1 To flatten a buckled shingle, squeeze some plastic roof cement under the buckle then weigh down the shingle with a brick or two for a couple of hours.

2 To remove a damaged shingle, grip its bottom edge (with gloves on) and wiggle it back and forth as you pull down. This will pull it free from the roofing nails that hold it in place.

3 Remove any exposed nails with a flat pry bar or a nail puller. If the roofing felt (the layer below the shingles) is damaged, repair the patch with some plastic roof cement.

4 Nail the new shingles in place, starting at the lowest course and working up. The new shingle will not be as faded as the old ones surrounding it. But over time the difference between the two will be less noticeable.

5 Before installing the last shingle, turn it over and apply a bead of plastic roof cement to the back top edge. Keep this bead about 1 in. below the top edge.

6 Carefully slide the last shingle into place. The plastic roof cement will smear across the underside of the shingle, which will improve the bond with the shingle below. Press the repair shingle flat, then lift up the shingle above and drive nails in the typical way.

7 If the damaged shingle falls in a roof valley, take it out and clean any old cement from the valley flashing. Then apply two beads of plastic roof cement along the edge of the valley.

8 Cut the repair shingle to size and slide it into position. Press it firmly into the valley cement to achieve the best bond.

Gas Grill
Tune-Up

19

Gas grills get grimy. Keep your faithful backyard cooking appliance running cleanly and efficiently by giving it a regular wash-up and tune-up.

WHAT'S BETTER THAN A GAS GRILL? Well, actually, quite a few things, including (according to some purists) a charcoal grill. Charcoal is supposed to deliver better flavor, higher temperatures, and a more authentic experience. With all these virtues stacked up against it, it's hard to understand why so many millions of people seem to prefer a gas grill. Maybe the gassers are just dumb.

Or maybe they like to walk out back, turn a valve, click a starter switch and be in business. Maybe they like getting nearly 500-degree temperatures without waiting for retirement. Or maybe it's the tank that lasts longer than a trunk load of charcoal, or the easy dishwasher clean up of so many parts. Just how dumb can they be?

Smart enough to understand that if you don't take care of a grill, it will start to fall apart? And once it does, you can either toss it and get your membership card in Disposal America punched, or you can pull together some time, tools, and simple replacement parts and get busy. The job breaks down into taking the grill apart, cleaning it up, then putting it back together with some new parts.

GAS GRILLS 101

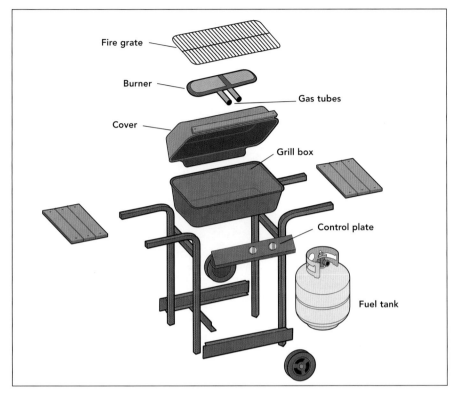

What's below the cooking grate depends on the make and model of the grill. Some grills have a fire grate at the bottom of the box with the burner on top of it. Alongside the burner are some lava rocks or ceramic briquettes, and on top of the burner is a drip plate that protects the burner from food and grease. Instead of lava rocks, some grills have porcelain-coated burner covers that retain heat. All of these parts except the burner can be lifted out. The burner is usually attached to the gas valve with a small pin that need pliers for removal. Sometimes the ends of a burner are screwed to the grill box. The igniter on some models is attached to the burner, so the wires going to the igniter switch must be removed. If the igniter on your grill is installed independent of the burner, just clean it in place.

TERMS YOU NEED TO KNOW

GAS MANIFOLD—A tube that joins two gas valves together. The supply hose from the gas storage tank is attached to the manifold.

GAS VALVE—The control valves for the gas supply. A knob mounted on the valve shaft turns the valve to increase or decrease gas flow, just like the burner knobs on a kitchen gas stove.

IGNITER—A piezoelectric device made of a mineral crystal that, when struck, generates a spark of electricity. This spark ignites the gas.

ELECTRODE—The part of the igniter that releases the spark. It is located in the gas stream and is connected to the igniter with wires.

DIFFICULTY LEVEL

This project can be completed in three to four hours.

HOW TO TUNE-UP A GAS GRILL

1 Check the gas hose from the tank to the gas valve manifold for any signs of wear. Bend it carefully and if you see any cracks or cuts, replace the hose.

2 Remove the clips or pins that hold the cover to the grill box, then lift off the cover. Clean it thoroughly with warm soapy water and a scouring pad, then set it aside to dry.

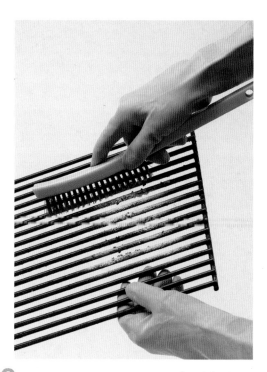

3 Remove the cooking grate and clean off the baked-on grime with a wire brush. Wash the grate with soapy water or oven cleaner. If it still looks bad, replace it.

4 Remove the burner tubes from the gas valve using pliers. Usually the two are joined with small clips. But sometimes the burner slips over the ends of the valves and is screwed to the grill box. In this case, just remove the screws.

Igniter switch

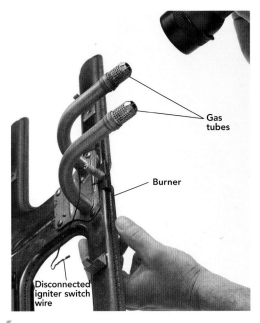

Gas tubes

Burner

Disconnected igniter switch wire

5 On some grills the igniter is mounted on the burner, so either the igniter has to be removed or the wires to the igniter switch must be removed. Once the burner is free, lift it out of the grill box.

6 Shine light down the gas tubes on the burner to check for insect nests. Spiders tend to congregate in these spots and restrict the flow of gas to the burner.

7 Clean any debris from the tubes using a bottle brush. Push it in slowly, turning it as you go. When the brush reaches the bottom of the tube, slowly pull it out. Then turn the burner over and shake out any debris. Repeat the process if you can still see debris in the tubes.

8 Flush out the burner with a garden hose and nozzle. Direct a stream of water into each tube. This should remove dust and other small debris from inside the burner. It also provides a way to check all the gas ports. If the water flows freely from each port then the burner is fine. But if some ports are clogged, use a small wire or a brass brush to loosen the clogs and open the ports.

Gas valve orifice

9 If your grill has removable gas valve orifices, take them out with an adjustable wrench and clean them with a toothbrush in warm soapy water. Dry them with a rag and thread them back into the gas valves.

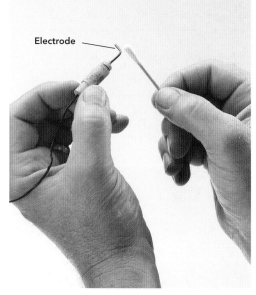

Electrode

10 Regardless of where the igniter electrode is located, clean it thoroughly with a cotton swab dipped in alcohol. If the igniter doesn't work or hasn't been working well, consider replacing it while the grill is disassembled.

11 Grill box walls almost always have heavy coats of grease and food residue on them. To remove this, use a putty knife or a paint scraper. Then wash the grill with soapy water and a garden hose. Because this job is so messy, it's best to do it out on the lawn where the grease won't stain things like the driveway or deck.

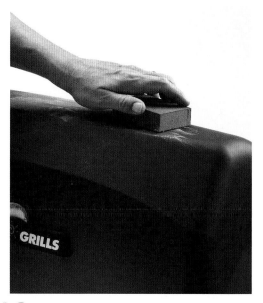

GRILLS

12 If the paint on the grill top is in bad shape, repaint it. Just remove any grease and grime, rough up the surface with 400-grit sandpaper or an abrasive pad, and wipe away the dust using a rag dipped in white vinegar. The vinegar will also take away any grease residue left behind from the washing earlier.

13 When the top is dry, spray on a couple coats of heat-resistant paint. Wait between applications as specified on the paint can. This is another thing you should do in the open air. Just wait for a calm day and wear a respirator.

14 If your grill has a fire grate, put it in the bottom of the grill box. Then, lower the burner into place and hook its gas tubes to the gas valves. If the burner has an igniter wire attached, make sure to feed this through its access hole (in the grill box) as you lower the burner into place.

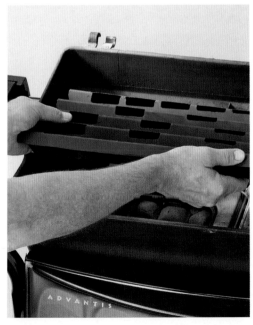

15 Once the burner is installed, replace the lava rocks or ceramic briquettes and cover the burner with the drip bar or bars. Drop the cooking grate into place and reattach the grill cover to the grill box.

Gas valve manifold

16 Attach the gas hose from the storage tank to the gas valve manifold, and turn on the gas. Check for leaks by painting a solution (one part dishwashing liquid and one part water) on all the fittings. If bubbles start to pop up, there's a leak. Tighten all the fittings and check with the solution again. Keep doing this until no bubbles appear.

Installing Landscape Lighting

20

Low-voltage lights are safe to install and use to beautify your outdoor spaces. Unlike solar landscape lights, they are powered by good old reliable electricity, so they really can stay on all night if you wish them to.

SOME LANDSCAPE LIGHTING MANUFACTURERS PITCH THEIR SYSTEMS AS SECURITY PRODUCTS. If you keep the outside of your house well lit, the reasoning goes, the thieves will turn elsewhere to find easier pickings. It's possible that the companies are right about this. But probably the stronger arguments are for improved safety and appearance.

It can't be surprising that adding some light to the dark makes going places safer. This idea has been around for a long time—a very long time. But the notion that you can improve the look of your house, by adding some nightlights, is more recent. In fact, decorating with exterior lights became widespread only in the last 25 years, when low-voltage landscape lighting showed up. The beauty of low-voltage lighting is that it can be installed by anyone without the risk of being shocked.

Low-voltage lights are powered by a transformer that steps 120-volt current down to a safe 12 volts. Choosing the location for the transformer is an important part of planning. You have two options: inside the house and outside the house. The outside installation is a little easier, but the inside one is a little better, especially from a security standpoint. Also take some time to review your light placement. Once you are happy with the plan, drive a small stake where you want each light to go.

LOW-VOLTAGE LIGHT KITS 101

Landscape lighting can be ordered in kit form or as individual pieces. Kits include a few light heads, some wire and a transformer that changes standard house current into low-voltage power. If you want half a dozen lights along the front walk, for example, then the kit is a good idea. It's cheaper, very easy to install and will last a long time unless the lights get run over by a lawnmower. Predictably, the individual parts approach offers a much wider range of light heads, a selection of transformers that can handle bigger jobs, and all the wire and other accessories anyone could need. Of course, this choice costs more money. A typical starter kit retails for about $150, while a collection of 20 expensive light heads, a big transformer and lots of wire can gobble up $1000 or more.

TERMS YOU NEED TO KNOW

LOW-VOLTAGE—Usually about 12 volts of current, instead of the standard 120 volts, used to power devices like outdoor landscape lights.

TRANSFORMER—A smaller version of the gray pods that are mounted at the top of electrical power poles. Changes current of one voltage to another. In this case, from the standard (and dangerous) 120-volt electrical service to a much safer 12-volt service.

TOOLS & SUPPLIES YOU NEED

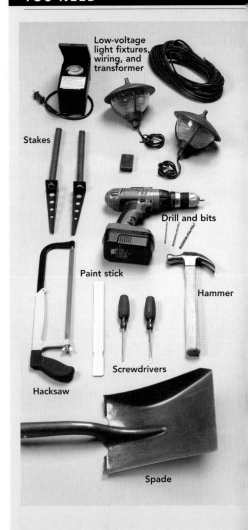

DIFFICULTY LEVEL

This project can be completed in eight to twelve hours.

HOW TO INSTALL LANDSCAPE LIGHTING

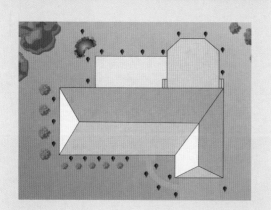

Make a diagram of your yard and mark the location of new fixtures. Note the wattages of the fixtures and use the diagram to select a transformer and plan the circuits.

1 Install your transformer or transformers. If you are installing one in a garage, mount it on a wall within 24" of the GFCI receptacle and at least 12" off the floor. If you are using an outdoor receptacle on a wall or a post, mount the transformer on the same post or an adjacent post at least 12" off the ground and not more than 24" inches from the receptacle. Do not use an extension cord.

2 Drill a hole through the wall or rim joist for the low-voltage cable and any sensors to pass through (inset). If a circuit begins in a high-traffic area, it's a good idea to protect the cable by running it through a short piece of PVC pipe or conduit and then into the shallow trench.

3 Attach the end of the low-voltage wire to the terminals on the transformer. Make sure that both strands of wire are held tightly by their terminal screws.

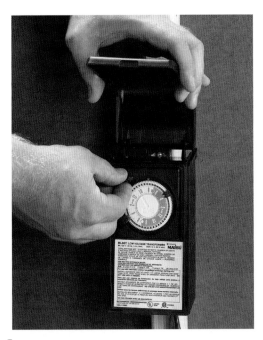

4 Transformers usually have a simple mechanism that allows you to set times for the lights to come ON and go OFF automatically. Set these times before hanging the transformer.

5 Many low-voltage light fixtures are modular, consisting of a spiked base, a riser tube and a lamp. On these units, feed the wires and the wire connector from the light section down through the riser tube and into the base.

6 Take apart the connector box and insert the ends of the fixture wire and the low voltage landscape cable into it. Puncture the wire ends with the connector box leads. Reassemble the connector box.

7 Feed the wire connector back into the light base and attach it according to directions that came with the lamp. In this model, all that was required was pushing the connector into a locking slot in the base.

HOW TO INSTALL LANDSCAPE LIGHTING

8 After the bulb is installed, assemble the fixture parts that cover it, including the lens cap and reflector.

9 Lay out the lights, with the wires attached, in the pattern you have chosen. Then cut the sod between fixtures with a spade. Push the blade about 5 in. deep and pry open a seam by rocking the blade back and forth.

10 Gently force the cable into the slot formed by the spade; don't tear the wire insulation. A paint stick (or a cedar shingle) is a good tool for this job. Push the wire to the bottom of the slot.

11 Firmly push the light into the slot in the sod. It the lamp doesn't seat properly, pull it out and cut another slot at a right angle to the first and try again.

12 Once the lamp is stabilized, tuck any extra wire into the slot using the paint stick. If you have a lot of extra wire, you can fold it and push the excess to the bottom of the slot. No part of the wire should be exposed when you are done with the job.

FIXTURE TIPS:

Specialty lights can cost a lot more than the standard plastic spike-base lamps. Because of this, many people modify the cheaper units to serve other purposes. To do this, first cut off the spike-base with a hacksaw.

To install a modified light on a deck, bore a wire-clearance hole through a deck board. Then feed the low-voltage wire through this hole and attach the base to the deck with screws. The same technique can be used to install modified units on planters or railings.

Many different specialty lights are available for use on a wood deck. This model mounts directly on the surface and the wires feed through an access hole under the light. Other lights that are thinner, but mount the same way, are designed for the underside of stair treads. These light up the stairs and reduce the chance of people stumbling in the dark.

You never know when you'll need to replace a door lockset or deadbolt,
but there are many situations when you'll be glad you know how to do it.

HOME SECURITY IS NOT SO MUCH A MATTER OF TENACIOUS CRIME PREVENTION
AS IT IS A QUESTION OF PEACE OF MIND. If you have been burglarized, you're bound
to feel vulnerable. So we all have an interest in keeping what's outside, outside. There are
many different approaches to accomplishing this, some cost a lot of money, some don't cost
much at all. The first (and most expensive) is having a whole-house security system installed
that notifies the police if there's any trouble. But not everyone needs or wants something so
involved. A more passive approach serves their needs. This generally means a combination
of motion-activated floodlights and quality door locks. When someone carefully approaches
a back door at night, there are few things as alarming as having a bright light suddenly flash
in their eyes. And there's nothing quite as discouraging as trying to break through a door
with a deadbolt lock when you want to go unnoticed. If you only care to do one of these
security building jobs, pick installing better locks. They're on the job every day, all day and all
night, whether the power is on or off.

LOCKSETS & DEADBOLTS 101

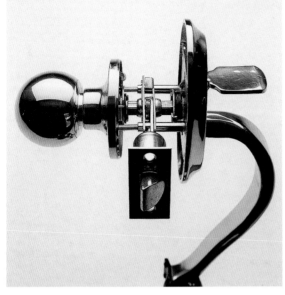

LOCKSETS—A good door deserves a good lockset. Inexpensive locksets are available for $10 to $15 and high quality ones cost around $40. Locksets for interior doors are called passage locks and are not suitable for exterior doors.

DEADBOLTS—A good deadbolt should cost around $25. There are several styles to choose from that differ in ways other than finish. Some are keyed on the outside and have a thumblatch on the interior side. If you have a glass sidelight or door panel, think about buying a model that's keyed on both the exterior and interior so an intruder can't break your glass and reach in to unlock the deadbolt.

TERMS YOU NEED TO KNOW

DOOR JAMB—Boards that define a door opening. The door hinges are hung on one jamb board and the strike plates for any locks are installed on the opposite jamb.

TEMPLATE—A pattern that establishes the proper layout for a procedure. In this case, a piece of paper taped to a door to indicate where clearance holes should be drilled.

LOCKSET—A complete locking system including knobs, locking mechanism, locking bolt, and decorative roses. Used on entry doors and interior doors where locking is desired.

DEADBOLT—A heavy-duty locking bolt that goes deep into the door jamb to prevent tampering.

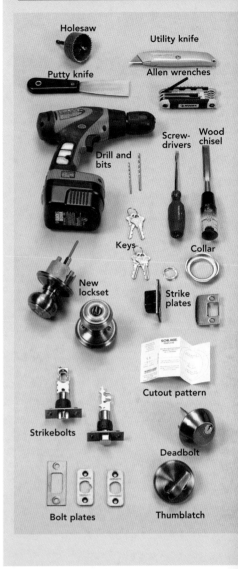

Holesaw

Utility knife

Putty knife

Allen wrenches

Drill and bits

Screw-drivers

Wood chisel

Keys

Collar

New lockset

Strike plates

Cutout pattern

Strikebolts

Deadbolt

Bolt plates

Thumblatch

DIFFICULTY LEVEL

SKILLS LEVEL

EASY   MODERATE

This project can be completed in two to three hours.

HOW TO INSTALL A LOCKSET

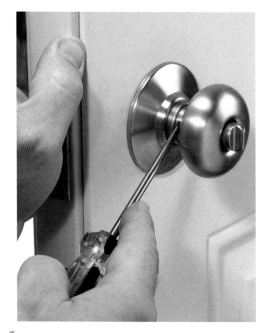

1 Remove the old lockset. The knob on the inside of the door is usually held in place with a small clip. This is located on the side of the sleeve that extends from the knob to the flange on the door surface. To release this clip, just push it into the flange with a screwdriver or an awl. Then pull off the knob.

2 Remove the flange next. These are usually snapped in place over the lock mechanism underneath. To remove one, just pry it off with a screwdriver pushed into a slot designed for it. Other flanges are held by small spring clips. By pushing down on the clip with a screwdriver, the flange can easily be pulled off with your fingers.

3 Once the flange is off, the lock mechanism will be accessible. The two sides of the lock are joined together by two screws. Remove these screws and take the lock components out of the lockset hole in the door.

4 With both sides of the lock removed, the lock bolt can be taken out. Remove the screws that hold the bolt plate to the edge of the door. Then pull out the bolt mechanism.

Bolt plate

5 Install the new bolt assembly and make sure that the screws in the bolt plate are driven tightly into the door. Separate the lock halves and slide them together with the door and bolt assembly sandwiched between.

6 While holding one side of the lock against the door, maneuver the other side of the lock so the screws fall in the slots made for them. Once the screw heads have cleared the slots, tighten the screws so both halves of the lock are tight against the door. Install the new knobs and new strike plate.

HOW TO INSTALL A DEADBOLT

TEMPLATE TIP

Many doors sold today come with holes for the lock-set predrilled. Some also are predrilled for a deadbolt, but very often you'll need to drill holes for the actual deadbolt you purchase. To assist in this, manufacturers provide a template that you tape to the door for reference. Following the manufacturer's instructions, tape the hole template to the door (make sure you've oriented the template to correspond to the actual thickness of your door) and mark the center point of each hole, including the bolt hole in the edge of the door. The deadbolt is usually located 7" or 8" above the lockset.

1 Determine the size of holesaw you need by checking the installation instructions that came with the lock. Then chuck this tool into a drill and bore the hole. Stop boring when the tip of the drill bit, at the center of the holesaw, breaks through the other side.

2 Go to the other side of the door and slide the pilot bit of the hole saw into the hole and cut out the rest of the waste material. If you try to cut through the door in a single pass, you risk tearing the steel covering (on steel-clad doors) as the hole-saw teeth break through the surface.

3 Drill the bolt hole through the edge of the door, using a spade bit or forstner bit. Make sure to keep the bit level so the bolt hole will enter the lock hole at the proper point.

4 Push the bolt assembly into the bolt hole so the bolt plate is flat on the edge of the door. Trace around the plate with a utility knife. Remove the mechanism and cut a ⅛"-deep mortise in the edge of the door with a sharp chisel (see next page).

5 Once you're satisfied with the fit, press the bolt plate into its mortise and attach it by driving in the two plate screws. Slide both sides of the lock into the bolt mechanism and attach them by driving the screws that hold the two parts together. Make sure these screws are tight. (inset).

MORTISING TECHNIQUE

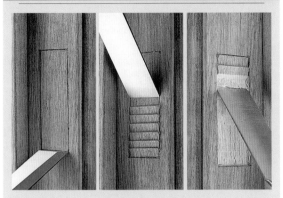

Installing hardware plates requires using a wood chisel to create a mortise for the hardware.

1 Deepen the outline for the mortise to ⅛" with a wood chisel (try to find a chisel the same width as the mortise). With the beveled face of the chisel blade facing into the mortise, rap the handle with a mallet.

2 Chisel a series of ⅛"-deep parallel cuts about ¼" apart.

3 Position the chisel bevel-side down at about a 45-degree angle. Strike with a mallet to chisel out the waste. Smooth the mortise bottom.

6 Extend the lock bolt and color its end with lipstick, a grease pencil, or a crayon. Then retract the bolt, close the door and extend the bolt so its end hits the jamb. This will yield the precise location of the bolt hole that's needed on the jamb. Drill a hole (usually 1½" deep) for the bolt with a spade bit (see installation instructions for actual hole size requirements).

7 Close the door and test the deadbolt to make sure the bolt fits into the bolt hole in the jamb. If not, enlarge the hole slightly. Once the bolt fits, center the strike plate over the bolt hole and trace it with a utility knife. Cut a mortise for the strike plate using a sharp chisel.

8 Finish up by installing the strike plate on the jamb. Some of these plates are oversized like the one above. But most look more like standard lockset strike plates. Both types, however, feature long screws that are driven through the jamb and deep into the wall studs behind.

Garage Door Tune-Up

22

A garage door that's well maintained and a working garage door opener are modern conveniences that are easy to take for granted.

IS THIS A GREAT COUNTRY OR WHAT? YOU'RE DRIVING HOME LATE AT NIGHT, IT'S POURING OUTSIDE, AND YOU'RE FREEZING BECAUSE YOU'VE GOT THE FLU. Then, you turn into your driveway, punch a little button, and your garage door opens, a light comes on, you pull in, and you're HOME. You didn't have to get drenched, or lift a door that felt like heavy metal, or scream at the heavens for making you so miserable. You danced away from all of this, and that is a good thing.

Unfortunately, over time, many good things become bad things, especially if they aren't well-maintained. And an overhead garage door is no exception. To keep everything running smoothly requires effort on three fronts: the door, the opener, and the electronic safety sensors that prevent the door from closing on cars, pets or people.

GARAGE DOORS 101

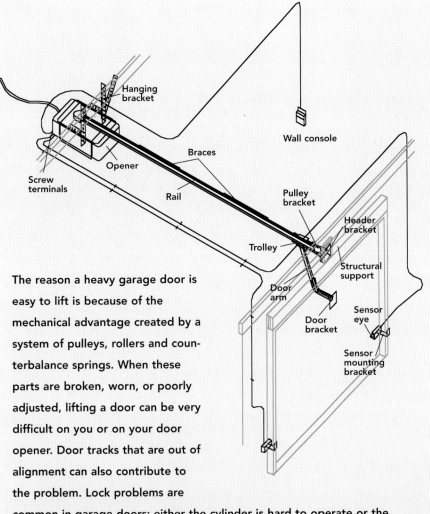

The reason a heavy garage door is easy to lift is because of the mechanical advantage created by a system of pulleys, rollers and counterbalance springs. When these parts are broken, worn, or poorly adjusted, lifting a door can be very difficult on you or on your door opener. Door tracks that are out of alignment can also contribute to the problem. Lock problems are common in garage doors: either the cylinder is hard to operate or the lock bar doesn't fit in its track opening.

Most door openers have a chain drive that may require tightening or lubrication. And sensors located on both sides of the door can be easily knocked out of alignment.

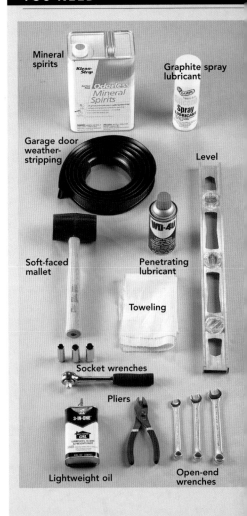

This project can be completed in four to eight hours.

TERMS YOU NEED TO KNOW

CHAIN-DRIVE OPENER—An electric opener that lifts and lowers a garage door with a chain that's driven by a motor mounted sprocket.

SCREW-DRIVE OPENER—An electric opener that lifts and lowers a garage door with a continuous screw that's driven by a gear in the motor.

CLOSING FORCE SENSITIVITY—This is a measurement of how quickly a garage door opener will stop and reverse the door's travel when an obstruction is sensed or hit.

HOW TO TUNE-UP A GARAGE DOOR

1 Begin the tune-up by lubricating the door tracks, pulleys and rollers. Use a lightweight oil, not grease, for this job. The grease catches too much dust and dirt.

2 Remove clogged or damaged rollers from the door by backing off the nuts that hold the roller brackets. The roller will come with the bracket when the bracket is pulled free.

3 Mineral spirits and kerosene are good solvents for cleaning roller bearings. Let the bearing sit for a half-hour in the solvent. Then brush away the grime build-up with an old paint brush or toothbrush.

4 If the rollers are making a lot of noise as they move over the tracks, the tracks are probably out of alignment. To fix this, check the tracks for plumb. If they are out of plumb the track mounting brackets must be adjusted.

5 To adjust out-of-plumb tracks, loosen all the track mounting brackets (usually 3 or 4 per track) and push the brackets into alignment.

6 It's often easier to adjust the brackets by partially loosening the bolts and tapping the track with a soft-faced mallet. Once the track is plumb, tighten all the bolts.

7 Sometimes the door lock bar opens sluggishly because the return spring has lost its tension. The only way to fix this is to replace the spring. One end is attached to the body of the lock; the other end hooks onto the lock bar.

8 If a latch needs lubrication, use graphite in powder or liquid form. Don't use oil because it attracts dust that will clog the lock even more.

9 Sometimes the lock bar won't lock the door because it won't slide into its opening on the door track. To fix this, loosen the guide bracket that holds the lock bar and move it up or down until the bar hits the opening.

10 Worn or broken weatherstripping on the bottom edge of the door can let in a lot of cold air and stiff breezes. Check to see if this strip is cracked, broken, or has holes along its edges. If so, remove the old strip and pull any nails left behind.

11 Measure the width of your garage door, then buy a piece of weatherstripping to match. These strips are standard lumber yard and home center items. Sometimes they are sold in kit form, with fasteners included. If not, just nail the stripping in place with galvanized roofing nails.

12 If the chain on your garage door opener is sagging more than ½" below the bottom rail, it can make a lot of noise and cause drive sprocket wear. Tighten the chain according to the directions in the owner's manual.

13 On openers with a drive screw instead of a chain, lubricate the entire length of the screw with lightweight oil. Do not use grease.

14 Test the door's closing force sensitivity and make adjustments at the opener's motor case if needed. Because both the sensitivity and the adjustment mechanism vary greatly between opener models, you'll have to rely on your owner's manual for guidance. If you don't have the owner's manual, you can usually download one from the manufacturer's website.

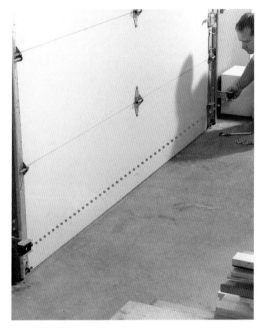

15 Check for proper alignment on the safety sensors near the floor. They should be pointing directly at one another and their lenses should be clean of any dirt and grease.

16 Make sure that the sensors are talking to the opener properly. Start to close the door, then put your hand down between the two sensors. If the door stops immediately and reverses direction, it's working properly. If it's not, make the adjustment recommended in the owner's manual. If that doesn't do the trick, call a professional door installer and don't use the door until it passes this test.

Tuning-Up
A Lawn Mower

23

Learning to do your own lawn mower maintenance will let you cut down
on big repair bills as you add years to the life of your machine.

A LAWN MOWER IS A WONDERFUL MACHINE, ESPECIALLY IF YOU LIKE CUTTING
GRASS. It does all the work while you take a stroll. Well, maybe not quite a stroll, but pushing a lawn mower isn't like carrying concrete blocks either. So a mower is wonderful because it works, and it's also wonderful because it's simple and reliable. In this day of picture phones and portable DVD players, it's nice to know that some technology from the 19th century is still around.

One of the beautiful simplicities of using a lawn mower is just how little maintenance it requires. By spending just a couple hours a year, a mower will last many years. And if you don't have time for a complete tune-up, nine times out of ten, some new gas and a new spark-plug will get you going, at least for a while. The rest of the good news is that a complete tune-up is cheap. About $20 should do the trick for most push mowers.

The complete tune-up has two parts: deck care and engine maintenance.

LAWNMOWERS 101

- Bail or operator control bar
- Rewind starter handle
- Handlebar
- Fuel cap
- Oil cap and oil dipstick
- Air cleaner
- Spark plug
- Side discharge cover
- Primer
- Wheel height adjustment
- Mower deck

Lawn mower maintenance falls into a few basic activites: small engine maintenace, sharpening blades, and cleaning/lubricating the deck and mower body and controls.

TERMS YOU NEED TO KNOW

AIR FILTER—This device is usually made of pleated paper and is designed to remove any dust or debris before the air reaches the carburetor. On most new machines the air filter is covered with a precleaner filter that keeps the major debris from getting to the air filter. This precleaner is easy to wash in soapy water, so it reduces the number of air filters that need to be replaced for the life of the mower.

FUEL FILTER—This small filter is installed in the gas line below the gas tank. It traps any debris in the gas before it gets to the carburetor. A fuel filter should be replaced when the mower is tuned-up.

CARBURETOR—This device blends the gas that comes from the fuel filter with the air that comes from the air filter, and passes this mixture into the engine cylinder for combustion.

CRANKCASE—This is the area at the bottom of a small engine that acts as a reservoir for the engine oil and protects the engine crankshaft.

GREASE FITTINGS—These are small pea-shaped metal fittings, located on the outside of various bearings, which have a small hole drilled through the center. When a grease gun hose is pushed over the end of this fitting, and the gun handle is squeezed, grease flows through the fitting and into the bearing that needs lubrication.

- Shop vac
- Small compressor or inflator
- Bench grinder
- Engine oil
- Garden hose
- Grease and grease gun
- Spark plug wrench
- Air filter
- Putty knife
- Siphon bulb
- Fuel filter
- Paint brush
- Cleaners and lubricants
- Pliers
- Socket wrenches
- Screwdrivers
- Metal files
- Drive belt

DIFFICULTY LEVEL

SKILLS LEVEL

EASY   MODERATE

This project can be completed in two hours.

HOW TO TUNE-UP A WALK-BEHIND LAWN MOWER

1 The first step is to remove the spark plug from the engine block. Once the plug is gone, the mower can't start while you are working on it.

2 Empty the gas from the tank with a siphon bulb or by turning over the mower (with the help of a friend) and letting the gas drain into a container. Dispose of the gas according to local ordinances for hazardous materials.

3 Lean the mower on its side and wash the underside of the deck with a garden hose. Thoroughly clean the wheels and make sure the wheel height adjustment mechanism works properly.

4 Remove stubborn grass from the deck with a putty knife. Eliminating the caked grass will improve the air movement under the deck and make the discharge of grass more efficient. The best approach to this job is to wash the deck after each cutting session, so the cut grass doesn't have a chance to build up.

5 Remove the blade by backing out the center bolt with a socket wrench or a box-end wrench. To keep the blade from turning when you turn the bolt, wedge a scrap wood block between the end of the blade and the deck. Sometimes you can just hold the blade with your other hand if the bolt isn't too stubborn. Be sure to wear heavy gloves when you try this.

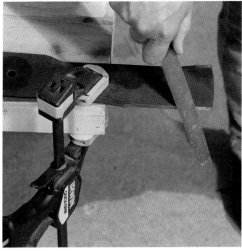

6 If the cutting edges on the blade are dull, but not chipped or severely dented, then sharpening with a file is all that's required. Maintain the angle that the manufacturer ground on the blade and remove the same amount of steel from both ends. If you file one end a lot more than the other, the blade will be out of balance and will vibrate when the mower is running.

7 If the blade has heavy damage, from hitting rocks and other debris on the lawn, then a bench grinder is the sharpening tool of choice. If you are not experienced using a grinder, it's better to take your blade to a sharpening shop or ask an experienced person to grind it. It's important to maintain the proper cutting angle and doing so on a grinder takes some practice.

8 Once the blade is removed, you'll have easy access to the oil drain plug. Remove this plug and let the used oil drain into a waste container. Some mowers don't have a drain plug. To remove the old oil you have to turn the mover over and let it drain from the fill hole. Have a friend help with the lifting and be careful to capture all the oil.

9 Replace the oil drain plug and reattach the cutting blade. Tighten both securely. Then turn the mower upright and check for smooth operation of all the controls. Most mowers will have a handle-mounted throttle and a brake lever of some kind. Some will have a separate choke cable. Lubricate these with a penetrating lubricant like WD-40. After each spray, work the handle back and forth to distribute the oil.

10 On most mowers, the engine cover hides the components that need servicing in a tune-up. To remove this cover, take out the screws that hold it in place. Put the screws in a safe place to avoid losing them.

11 Once the cover is off, brush away any debris from the top of the engine with an old paintbrush. Then vacuum up the loose material. Lawn mowers are built to work in dusty and dirty conditions. But if mowers are kept clean, this reduces the chance that foreign matter will get into the carburetor and keep the engine from starting or running smoothly.

12 Remove the air filter cover by backing out the screw or twisting off the wing nut that holds it in place. Under the cover should be a paper air filter surrounded by a foam precleaner filter. Remove the precleaner, then inspect the paper filter. If it's dirty, it should be cleaned with compressed air or replaced. Because maintenance is always easy to put off, if you've gotten this far you might as well replace the filter. You can't be sure when you'll get back.

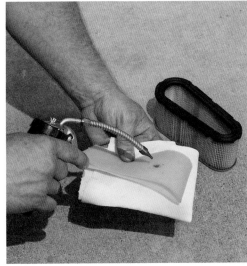

Option: If your mower has a foam precleaner filter for the air filter, remove it and wash it in warm soapy water. Then rinse the precleaned repeatedly until you can't see any soap bubbles when you squeeze it. When the foam is dry, soak it with new oil, squeeze out the excess and put the precleaner back in place.

13 The fuel system is the most vulnerable component of a mower's engine. This is largely because old gas can leave harmful deposits in the carburetor ports and on the walls of the fuel bowl. Debris can also be trapped in the bowl and be drawn into the carburetor, which can plug things up. To gain access, remove the nut from the bottom of the bowl and pull the bowl off the carburetor carefully. Pour out the gas and wipe away any debris.

14 Clean the carburetor and ports with spray carburetor cleaner. This is a common auto parts store product. Just spray the walls and the ports until they look clean. If you're spraying this cleaner outside, you don't need a mask. But if you're inside a closed garage, wear one.

15 Locate the fuel filter in the rubber fuel line that comes out of the bottom of the fuel tank. This filter is usually held in place with a couple of spring clamps. Just compress and slide the clamps back, take out the old filter, put in a new one and reset the clamps.

16 Buy the recommended spark plug for your mower and install it with the plug wrench that came with the mower. You can also use a regular socket wrench but these aren't always deep enough to reach all the way into the socket. No matter what is used, take care not to over-tighten the plug. It's easy to strip the block threads and fixing this problem is expensive. Just tighten the plug until it seats. Then make only another ¼ turn.

17 Fill the crankcase with new oil and put fresh gas in the tank. Then push the wire onto the end of the spark plug and try to start the engine. It should fire right away. However, sometimes it takes a few pulls to get the gas from the tank into the carburetor.

HOW TO TUNE-UP A LAWN TRACTOR

LAWN TRACTORS

Tuning-up a lawn tractor isn't much different than tuning-up a push mower, at least when it comes to the engine. But tractors have other components that need attention. The first is the tires. You should maintain the specified inflation pressure to get the best wear and best ride from the machine. And there are a few more controls to keep lubricated, like the levers for the PTO (power take-off) and the deck lifting mechanism.

Maintaining the mowing deck is different for a tractor because the deck is bigger and not attached directly to the engine. The deck is suspended below the tractor and is powered by a drive belt that is hooked to a pulley on the engine. This drive belt should be inspected once a year for worn edges and cracks. Also, you must remove the deck once a year to clean it, sharpen the blade (or blades) and grease any bearings.

1 Keep tractor tires inflated to the recommended pressure. This will improve the ride and the performance of the tractor while getting the most wear out of the tires. To do this job, you need a compressor, which isn't the high-ticket item it used to be. Large building centers, for example, sell small compressor for about $60, and simple electric tire inflators can be found in the $40 range.

2 Clean all the controls on the dash and fender of the tractor, then lubricate them with a penetrating spray lubricant like WD-40. After spraying, move the deck lift lever up and down several times to disperse the lubricant.

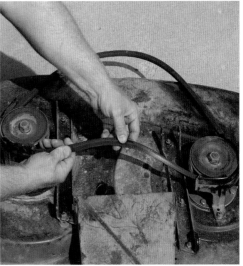

3 Check the mower drive belt for signs of frayed or cracked edges. If it looks warn, replace it. The owner's manual will show how to remove and reinstall a belt and how to adjust the new belt's tension for the best performance.

4 When the deck blade is off for sharpening, look for any grease fittings that lubricate the blade shafts. Sometimes these are under the deck and sometimes they're above it. Fill these fittings with grease using a grease gun. Be sure to wipe the fitting clean before hooking on the gun hose.

5 Once the deck is cleaned and the blade sharpened and reinstalled, reattach the deck to the mower. Then take the time to level the deck, which is almost always easy as long as you work on a flat surface. After the deck is leveled, adjust the wheels to match the cutting height you desire. The owner's manual will describe the specifics for your mower. Generally, if the grass is cut higher, the grass will be healthier.

Installing
A Storm Door

24

A quality storm door helps seal out cold drafts, keeps rain and snow off your entry door, and lets a bug-free breeze into your home when you want one.

STORM DOORS PROTECT THE ENTRY DOOR FROM DRIVING RAIN OR SNOW. They create a dead air buffer between the two doors that acts like insulation. When the screen panels are in place, the door provides great ventilation on a hot day. And, they deliver added security, especially when outfitted with a lockset and a deadbolt lock.

If you want to install a brand new storm door or replace an old one that's seen better days, your first job is to go shopping. Storm doors come in many different styles to suit just about anyone's design needs. And they come in different materials, including aluminum, vinyl, and even fiberglass. (Wood storm doors are still available but not in preassembled form.) All these units feature a pre-hung door in a frame that is mounted on the entry door casing boards. Depending on the model you buy, installation instructions can vary. So be sure to check the directions that came with your door before starting the job.

STORM DOORS 101

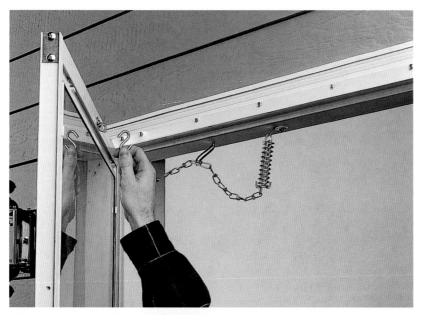

TOOLS & SUPPLIES YOU NEED

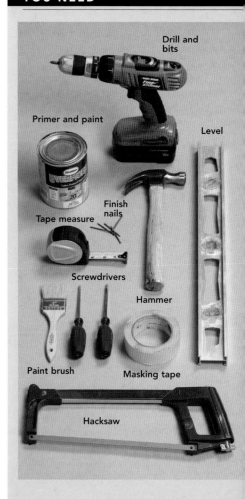

Drill and bits

Primer and paint

Level

Finish nails

Tape measure

Screwdrivers

Hammer

Paint brush

Masking tape

Hacksaw

DIFFICULTY LEVEL

SKILLS LEVEL

EASY   MODERATE

This project can be completed in six to eight hours.

DOOR CLOSERS—Storm doors are relatively lightweight and because they open outward they are susceptible to catching the wind and becoming damaged. For this reason, a storm door should be equipped with a spring-protected safety chain at the top and a pneumatic closer that can be located anywhere on the door (usually about handle level).

TERMS YOU NEED TO KNOW

DOOR JAMBS—The boards that line the rough opening of the doorway. The door swings between them and the hinges and strike plate are mounted on them.

DOOR CASING BOARDS—Boards that are nailed to the jambs and the wall surrounding any door opening. They lay flat against the wall covering inside, and flat against the wall sheathing on the outside.

HOW TO INSTALL A STORM DOOR

1 Test fit the door in the opening. If it is loose, add a shim to the hinge side of the door. Cut the piece with a circular saw and nail it to the side of the jamb, flush with the front of the casing.

2 Install the rain cap at the top of the door opening. The directions for the door you have will explain exactly how to do this. Sometimes it's the first step, like we show here; sometimes it's installed after the door is in place.

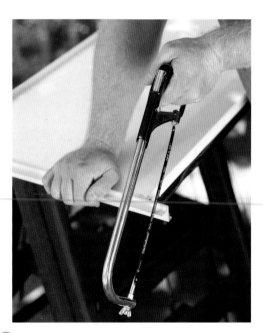

3 Measure the height of the opening and cut the hinge flange to match this measurement. Use a hacksaw and work slowly so the saw won't hop out of the cut and scratch a visible area of the hinge.

4 Lift the door and push it tightly into the opening. Partially drive one mounting screw near the bottom and another near the top. Check the door for plumb, and when satisfied, drive all the mounting screws tight to the flange.

5 Measure from the doorway sill to the rain cap to establish the length of the latch-side mounting flange.

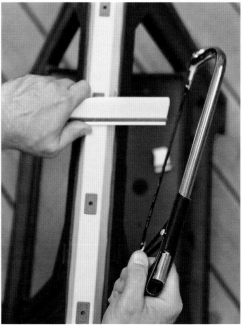

6 Cut the latch-side flange with a hacksaw. Work carefully so you don't pull out the weather-stripping from the flange channel as you cut.

7 Install the latch-side flange with a couple of partially-driven screws. Then check that the opening width is the same at the top, middle and bottom. When you're satisfied that this flange is parallel to the hinge flange, install all the mounting screws securely.

8 To install the door sweep, slide it over the bottom of the door and install its mounting screws loosely. Make sure the sweep forms a tight seal with the sill, then tighten the screws.

9 Install the lockset by pushing the outside half of the unit into the mounting holes from the outside of the door. Hold it in place with masking tape.

10 Mount the other half of the lockset on the inside of the door. Just line up the screws and push them into the threaded tubes on the outside half of the unit. Tighten the screws securely.

11 Install the deadbolt in the same way you installed the lockset. Slide the outside half in first and then add the inside half and tighten the mounting screws.

12 Install the strike plates for both the lockset (shown here) and the deadbolt locks. These plates are just screwed to the door jamb where the lock bolt and deadbolt fall (see pages 106 to 111).

13 Begin installing the door closer by screwing the jamb bracket in place. Most of these brackets have slotted screw holes so you can make minor adjustments without taking off the bracket.

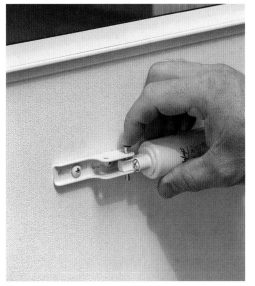

14 Install the door closer bracket on the inside of the door. Then mount the closer on the jamb bracket and the door bracket. Usually the closer is attached to these with some form of short locking pin.

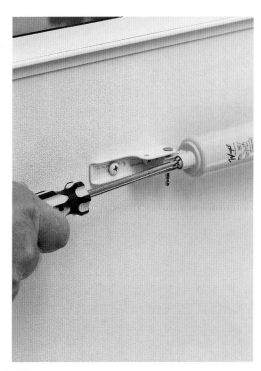

15 Adjust the automatic door closer so it closes the door completely without slamming it. The adjustment is usually made by turning a set screw in and out with a screwdriver.

16 Some doors feature a storage compartment for the glass sash and the screen sash between the bottom panels of the door. To change sashes, just unlock one and slide it down. Then pull up the other and lock it in place.

25

Installing House Gutters

Installing a snap-together vinyl gutter system is a manageable task for most do-it-yourselfers. Before you purchase new gutters, create a detailed plan and cost estimate. Include all the necessary parts, not just the gutter and drain pipe sections; they make up only part of the total system. Test-fit all the pieces on the ground before you begin the actual installation.

GUTTERS PREVENT RUNOFF FROM YOUR ROOF THAT CAN DAMAGE FOUNDATION PLANTINGS. THEY HELP KEEP WATER OUT OF YOUR BASEMENT, AND THEY REDIRECT WATER AWAY FROM ENTRYWAYS. In short, there are plenty of good reasons to install gutters on a house that doesn't have a gutter system, or to replace a failing gutter system. However, be aware that installing new gutters in cold climates can be a real problem. (As the old saying goes: You can't live with them and you can't live without them.) They have a bad rep because they cause so many ice dams. Without gutters, this water would just run off the edge of the roof. So consider all the pluses and minuses carefully before investing in a gutter system. If you decide to go for it, here's one tip: When calculating the costs, don't be fooled by the relatively low per-foot cost for a run of gutter or downspouts, since it's the fittings and connectors that make up most of the cost of DIY gutter installations.

GUTTERS 101

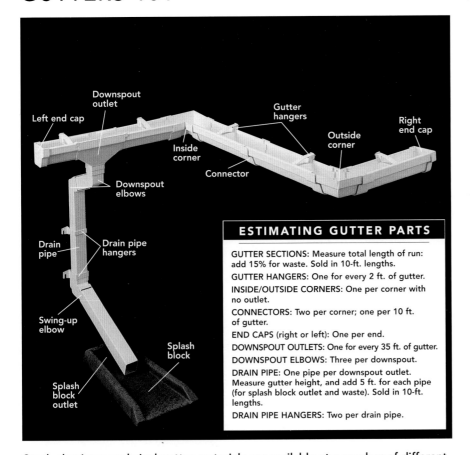

Left end cap
Downspout outlet
Inside corner
Downspout elbows
Gutter hangers
Outside corner
Connector
Right end cap
Drain pipe
Drain pipe hangers
Swing-up elbow
Splash block
Splash block outlet

ESTIMATING GUTTER PARTS

GUTTER SECTIONS: Measure total length of run: add 15% for waste. Sold in 10-ft. lengths.

GUTTER HANGERS: One for every 2 ft. of gutter.

INSIDE/OUTSIDE CORNERS: One per corner with no outlet.

CONNECTORS: Two per corner; one per 10 ft. of gutter.

END CAPS (right or left): One per end.

DOWNSPOUT OUTLETS: One for every 35 ft. of gutter.

DOWNSPOUT ELBOWS: Three per downspout.

DRAIN PIPE: One pipe per downspout outlet. Measure gutter height, and add 5 ft. for each pipe (for splash block outlet and waste). Sold in 10-ft. lengths.

DRAIN PIPE HANGERS: Two per drain pipe.

Steel, aluminum and vinyl gutter materials are available at a number of different outlets, including lumber yards, home centers and some hardware stores. To make a shopping list, first measure the length of gutter you need. Then calculate the amount of downspout required (generally sold in 10-ft. lengths.) A good rule of thumb for 5-in. gutters says that any gutter run less than 40 ft. only needs one downspout. For longer ones, a downspout should be installed at both ends of the run. After you total up the gutters and downspouts, list the fittings. Each downspout requires an outlet fitting, and both ends of the completed gutter need an end cap. Any joints need a splice fitting, and any inside or outside corners need inside or outside corner fittings. Two elbows are required to make the transition between the outlet fitting and its downspout. And two fastener brackets are needed for each section of downspout. You'll also need hanging brackets for the gutters. Buy enough to install one every 2 ft.

TERMS YOU NEED TO KNOW

GUTTER PITCH—This is the amount that a gutter slopes from its high to low points, usually expressed as difference in height per 10 ft. of run.

GUTTER RUN—The gutter sections and fittings that fall between gutter end caps.

TOOLS & SUPPLIES YOU NEED

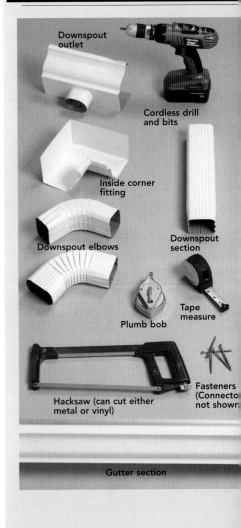

Downspout outlet
Cordless drill and bits
Inside corner fitting
Downspout elbows
Downspout section
Plumb bob
Tape measure
Hacksaw (can cut either metal or vinyl)
Fasteners (Connecto not shown

Gutter section

DIFFICULTY LEVEL

SKILLS LEVEL

EASY   MODERATE

This project can be completed in two to four days.

HOW TO INSTALL VINYL GUTTERS

1 Mark a point at the high end of each gutter run, 1" from the top of the fascia. Snap chalk lines that slope toward downspouts. For runs longer than 35 ft., mark a slope from a high point in the center toward downspouts at each end.

2 Install downspout outlets near the ends of gutter runs (at least one outlet for every 35 ft. of run). The tops of the outlets should be flush with the slope line, and they should align with end caps on the corners of the house, where drain pipes will be attached.

3 Following the slope line, attach hangers or support clips for hangers for a complete run. Attach them to the fascia at 24" intervals, using deck screws.

4 Following the slope line, attach outside and inside corners at all corner locations that don't have end caps.

5 Use a hacksaw to cut gutter sections to fit between outlets and corners. Attach the end caps and connect the gutter sections to the outlets. Cut and test-fit gutter sections to fit between outlets, allowing for expansion gaps.

6 Join the gutter sections together, using connectors. Attach gutter hangers to the gutter (for models with support clips mounted on the fascia). Hang the gutters, connecting them to the outlets.

7 Cut a section of drain pipe to fit between two downspout elbows. One elbow should fit over the tail of the downspout outlet and the other should fit against the wall. Assemble the parts, slip the top elbow onto the outlet, and secure the other to the siding with a drain pipe hanger.

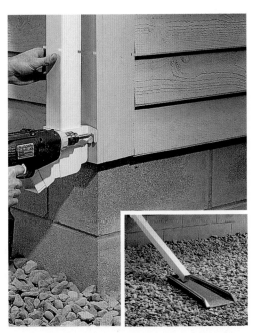

8 Cut a piece of drain pipe to fit between the elbow at the top of the wall and the end of the drain pipe run, staying at least 12" above the ground. Attach an elbow, and secure the pipe to the wall with a drain pipe hanger. Add accessories, such as splash blocks, to help channel water away from the house (inset).

26

Repairing Stucco

Small stucco problems rarely turn into major problems—if you catch them when they are still small. A caulk product designed for masonry will fix small stucco woes. The patched area can then be covered with touch-up paint so that it blends in.

STUCCO IS ONE OF THE MOST DURABLE SIDING MATERIALS USED ON HOMES. But damp climates can be especially hard on these surfaces, and if left unattended, small cracks can lead to some pretty big problems. A few years of water damage can cause large sections of stucco to loosen and even fall away from your house.

Fortunately, these problems aren't all that hard to repair, even for beginners. And keeping stucco in good condition is one of the easiest maintenance tasks of all. All you really need to do is inspect your stucco once each year and fill any small cracks you find—which won't happen that often. But let's say you forgot, and your stucco has a more major problem. Don't panic; just keep reading.

STUCCO 101

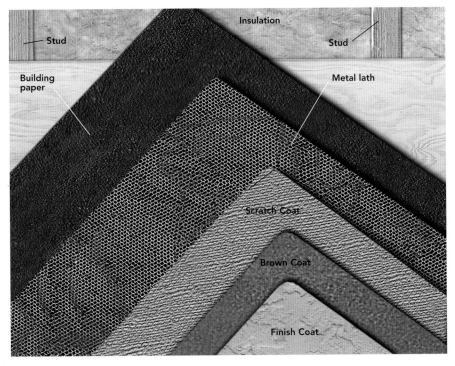

- Stud
- Insulation
- Stud
- Building paper
- Metal lath
- Scratch Coat
- Brown Coat
- Finish Coat

Your original stucco walls were made from three layers of cement-based stucco laid over a metal fabric, called lathe, which is nailed over the building paper and plywood or plank sheathing covering the skeleton of the walls. Today, though, you can just use a single premixed stucco product, sold in plastic buckets, to make repairs to stucco.

TERMS YOU NEED TO KNOW

BROWN COAT—The second of three stucco layers, the brown coat uses the same formulation as the scratch coat, but is applied in a smooth layer.

SCRATCH COAT —The first of three layers of stucco, it earns its name because it is scored with grooves while still wet so that the following coats will adhere to it.

FINISH COAT—The top layer of stucco, which is often tinted and textured to provide a decorative finish.

METAL LATH—This porous steel fabric is nailed to wall sheathing to provide the base for the first, or scratch coat of stucco.

SQUARE-END TROWEL—a straight, smooth metal tool used to apply stucco and other masonry substances.

- Type M mortar
- Stucco mix
- Drip screed
- Self-furring expanded metal lath
- Metal edging
- Hammer stapler
- Staples
- Building paper
- Mortar tint
- Roofing nails

DIFFICULTY LEVEL

SKILL LEVEL

EASY   MODERATE

This project can be completed in two to four days.

HOW TO PATCH STUCCO

1 Remove loose material from the repair area, using a wire brush. If the underlying metal lath has any rust, brush this away, too.

2 Use a broad putty knife or small trowel to apply premixed stucco repair compound to the repair area, with enough depth to slightly overfill the depression.

3 Smooth out the repair area with your knife or trowel, taking care to make the borders of the repair blend smoothly into the surrounding wall surface. Use a whisk broom or trowel to duplicate the texture of the wall.

4 If you have any bigger patch areas, chip away the loose stucco, cut away the loose metal lath, then cut and attach new lath to the wall sheathing.

5 If your large patch area includes a corner, cut and install a piece of metal edging along the corner of the wall. Sheet metal is sharp, so make sure you wear gloves and eye protection when cutting it.

6 Apply a base, or scratch coat of premixed stucco compound over the lath, with a thickness of about 3/8". Score closely spaced horizontal lines in the wet surface, using a scratching tool or a nail. Let the stucco dry for a couple of days.

7 Apply the second coat of stucco patch compound, to withing 1/4" of the original surface. Let the patch dry for a day or two.

8 Apply the final coat of stucco, then texture it to match the surrounding wall, using a whisk broom or trowel. After the stucco dries, you can either paint the patch area to match the surrounding wall, or paint the entire wall for nearly invisible blend.

Metric Equivalents

Inches (in.)	1/64	1/32	1/25	1/16	1/8	1/4	3/8	2/5	1/2	5/8	3/4	7/8	1	2	3	4	5	6	7	8	9	10	11	12	36	39.4
Feet (ft.)																								1	3	3½
Yards (yd.)																									1	1½
Millimeters (mm)	0.40	0.79	1	1.59	3.18	6.35	9.53	10	12.7	15.9	19.1	22.2	25.4	50.8	76.2	101.6	127	152	178	203	229	254	279	305	914	1,000
Centimeters (cm)							0.95	1	1.27	1.59	1.91	2.22	2.54	5.08	7.62	10.16	12.7	15.2	17.8	20.3	22.9	25.4	27.9	30.5	91.4	100
Meters (m)																								.30	.91	1.00

Converting Measurements

TO CONVERT:	TO:	MULTIPLY BY:
Inches	Millimeters	25.4
Inches	Centimeters	2.54
Feet	Meters	0.305
Yards	Meters	0.914
Miles	Kilometers	1.609
Square inches	Square centimeters	6.45
Square feet	Square meters	0.093
Square yards	Square meters	0.836
Cubic inches	Cubic centimeters	16.4
Cubic feet	Cubic meters	0.0283
Cubic yards	Cubic meters	0.765
Pints (U.S.)	Liters	0.473 (Imp. 0.568)
Quarts (U.S.)	Liters	0.946 (Imp. 1.136)
Gallons (U.S.)	Liters	3.785 (Imp. 4.546)
Ounces	Grams	28.4
Pounds	Kilograms	0.454
Tons	Metric tons	0.907

TO CONVERT:	TO:	MULTIPLY BY:
Millimeters	Inches	0.039
Centimeters	Inches	0.394
Meters	Feet	3.28
Meters	Yards	1.09
Kilometers	Miles	0.621
Square centimeters	Square inches	0.155
Square meters	Square feet	10.8
Square meters	Square yards	1.2
Cubic centimeters	Cubic inches	0.061
Cubic meters	Cubic feet	35.3
Cubic meters	Cubic yards	1.31
Liters	Pints (U.S.)	2.114 (Imp. 1.76)
Liters	Quarts (U.S.)	1.057 (Imp. 0.88)
Liters	Gallons (U.S.)	0.264 (Imp. 0.22)
Grams	Ounces	0.035
Kilograms	Pounds	2.2
Metric tons	Tons	1.1

Converting Temperatures

Convert degrees Fahrenheit (F) to degrees Celsius (C) by following this simple formula: Subtract 32 from the Fahrenheit temperature reading. Then, mulitply that number by 5/9. For example, 77°F - 32 = 45. 45 × 5/9 = 25°C.

To convert degrees Celsius to degrees Fahrenheit, multiply the Celsius temperature reading by 9/5. Then, add 32. For example, 25°C × 9/5 = 45. 45 + 32 = 77°F.

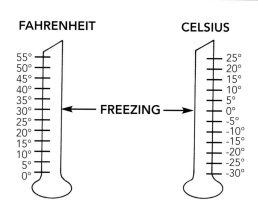

INDEX

INDEX (CONTINUED)

*A*lso from
CREATIVE PUBLISHING INTERNATIONAL

More Black & Decker 101 titles

Projects You Really Can Do Yourself

The course catalog for our popular new 101 book series is growing fast. We're pleased to offer four additional texts that are aimed specifically at the beginning do-it-yourselfer. Each beautifully photographed book features at least 25 well-selected projects in the subjects you'll need to study the most. *Decorating 101* shows you how to paint just about every surface in your home, along with other common home decorating projects, like hanging curtains and window shades. *Flooring 101* will teach you how to maintain every type of floor and fix those pesky flooring problems yourself. And for the first-time homeowner, *Wiring 101* and *Plumbing 101* are the ultimate in handy reference books, put together the *101* way. Enroll today.

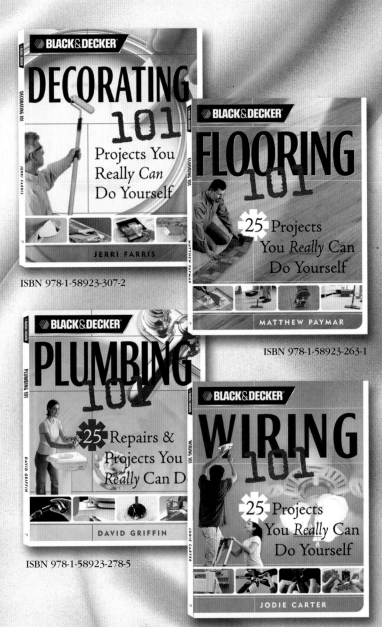

ISBN 978-1-58923-307-2

ISBN 978-1-58923-263-1

ISBN 978-1-58923-278-5

ISBN 978-1-58923-246-4

CREATIVE PUBLISHING INTERNATIONAL
18705 LAKE DRIVE EAST
CHANHASSEN, MN 55317
WWW.CREATIVEPUB.COM

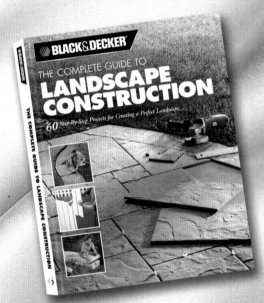
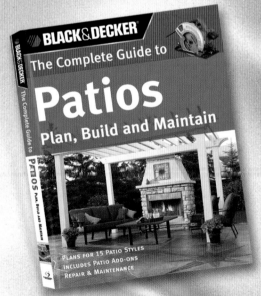